THE CHRISTIAN WITCH'S HANDBOOK

Solitary Practitioner's Edition

H. Fuller Hutchinson

PublishAmerica
Baltimore

© 2010 by H. Fuller Hutchinson.
All rights reserved. No part of this book may be reproduced, stored in a retrieval system or transmitted in any form or by any means without the prior written permission of the publishers, except by a reviewer who may quote brief passages in a review to be printed in a newspaper, magazine or journal.

First printing

PublishAmerica has allowed this work to remain exactly as the author intended, verbatim, without editorial input.

ISBN: 978-1-4489-5101-7
PUBLISHED BY PUBLISHAMERICA, LLLP
www.publishamerica.com
Baltimore

Printed in the United States of America

This book is dedicated to Jesus the Christ, Larry, Finnian, and to every Christian Witch who has been before and to those who will come after.

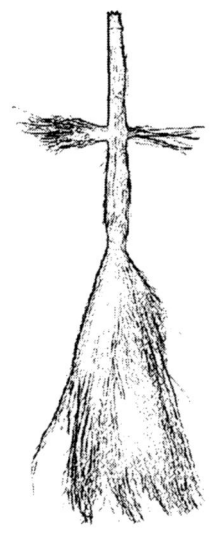

Dear Reader,

This book is written to give form and encouragement to the "witchy way" of worshiping Christ. No matter what I have written here, please study for yourself, let God guide you, and make your own choices, create your worship and your opinions based on your relationship to Him.

Brightest Blessings,
Hilea

Contents

Introduction to Christian Witchery *11*
    Jesus and Magic 14
    Christian Witch's Creed 16
    What Christian Witchery is Not 18
    Handling Criticism with Grace 20

Worship *23*
    Baptism (Your Dedication to Christ) 24
    Communion (The Lord's Supper) 25
    Personal and Family Alters 26
    Holidays/Holy Days: The Wheel of the Year 27
    The Lunar Calendar 38

Bubble, Bubble, Toil and Trouble…(Shakespeare)
    The "Crafting" of Prayers *41*
    Praying Spells/Casting Prayers 41
    Casting Circles…Sacred Space 43
    "Cleansing" and "Charging" Items for
        Prayer/Spell Purposes 45
    Tools of the Craft 46
    The Wisdom of the Mage: A Formula for Magic 48
    My Basic Formula for Casting a Prayer/Spell 49
    Prayer/Spells 50

Potions *52*
    Teas 52
    Tinctures 55
    Oils 56

Powders *58*
   Positive Energy Powder 60

Charms *61*

Charts *64*
   Element Chart 64
   Herbal Energy Chart: Magic Only 64
   Color Energy Chart 68
   Crystal Energy/Conductivity Chart 71
   Casting Template 73

More "Witchy" Ways *74*
   Candle Magic 74
   Knot Magic 76
   Cauldron Magic 77
   Stitching Magic 78
   Touch Magic 80
   Drawing Down the Moon 82
   Drinking in the Sun 83

More Prayer/Spells *84*
   Home Blessing 84
   "Restore the Energy" Balance Spell 85
   The Halloween "Letting Go" Ritual 85
   Thieving Key Spell 86
   A "Deep Struggle" Prayer for Another 87
   Clarity of Problem Candle 88
   Bless and Bind an Evil Enemy 88
   Create a Harmonious Home 89
   Protect a Furry Friend 90
   Joy Candle 91

Bless a Garden	91
Bless a New Home	92
Charmed Hair Ties for a Little Girl	92
Reverse the Curse Spell	93
Witch's Bottle for Household Blessings	94
Spring Blessings Cauldron Spell	94
Poetry	95

Working with Others 97
    Christian Witch's Circle 100

Christian Witch's Glossary 114

Frequently Asked Questions 120

Bibliography 124

Prologue

The idea for this book came about because I couldn't find one that honored both magic and Christ, let alone one that honored the natural (and supernatural) magic *of* Christ. Nor could I find one that gave any direction as to how to do this. Not surprising, given the amount of condemnation and hypocrisy heaped upon the concepts of magic by many western religions. There is no polarity between using natural magic created by God and the Messiah himself, but there is a definite conflict between natural magic and (drum roll, please…) the "church". This is especially prevelant in those church groups who believe that the Bible is the "end all, be all" rule of judgment regarding humanity, instead of the Living God. These people are having a relationship with a book and not the God of that book.

Christian religion has often hi-jacked magic for its own use, and largely condemned any magical concept that may present any perceived threat to the establishment. In effect, they have taken the living, eternal magic of Jesus, which is the magic of God, and hidden it in liturgy, theology, prayer cloths, anointing oils, power of positive thinking, name it/claim it theology, and Christian ritual, then adapted it to the new corporate standards that we now call church.

I have no problem with the gathering together to worship and learn more about the Lord, but the true power of God is seldom in it. God is often deeply buried in a humanistic corporation based on man's concept of self importance and humanistic order. I don't accept that...I believe that Jesus empowers all Christians to walk in a personal relationship with God, and came to save all the people who are willing. Jesus has a place in this world for us all.

But because of all this, coming out of the "broom" closet is not easy for a Christian Witch...or any witch, for that matter. We are a different breed, not unlike the early American witches of the Salem area, or those Christian witches of Western Europe who were hanged and burned at the stake. And yes, some of them really were witches, but few of them were probably evil, and none of them were Wiccan. Probably few of them even labeled themselves as witches, but many were people who practiced the natural healing magics of midwifery and "wort-cunning" for themselves, their family and neighbors and...they were Christians.

Nowadays, I often tell people who make an issue about my beliefs that, "Yes, I'm way to "witchy" for most Christians, and way to "Christian" for most witches!" Humor always seems to take the edge off that sword of condemnation, wielded deftly by the person standing there before me who, by that time, is wondering if I'm some sort of Satan worshiper, or maybe an escapee from the local sanitarium.

So this book is written for everybody: The Christians, The Wiccans, the people who suspect that they are somehow magical beings, and those who know they are and love the Lord for making them such. But most of all, it's written for the Christian Witches who are looking for a home. You are not alone.

Introduction to Christian Witchery

Being a Christian Witch takes courage, derived from faith. Some of us are born with "witchy" magics like psychic intuition, the ability to talk to trees, or see ghosts. These are spiritual gifts given by God, and should only be used in serving His purpose. Sometimes, even extra-sensory perception is naturally "built in" through benign brain growths that over-activate the pineal gland or is even developed through brain or psychological traumas.

Often, this "witchiness" runs in family lines due to genetic anomalies. Some genetic anomalies, also called markers, are even being documented in some families through "genetic" testing to genealogically trace family heritage, including mine: the Fuller family line in America.

So, if you suspect yourself of being rather "witchy" then here's a simple test:

Do you feel a deep spiritual connection with nature and God, or God in nature?

Do you have any extra-sensory perceptions, like that deep feeling in your gut about something that is about to happen, both good and bad?

Do you refuse to fit the role of women as described by Paul in the Bible, even though you've tried your best?

Do you ever feel a special connection to the moon and her cycles?

Do you know that deep within is a warrior of Christ, a healer, or something "more" just waiting to get out?

Do you feel good barefoot and often curl up into chairs like a cat?

Do you know that you believe in Jesus Christ, but feel that there's something the local church isn't telling you?

Do you know of any documented or accused witches in your family tree?

Do you have an unquenchable curiosity about all things magic?

Do you suspect that there's a "female" side of God, too?

If you have answered "yes" to the majority of these questions, then you may be a Christian Witch, and may have been given very special gifts from God. We sometimes come to understand that these gifts are the true magics, still alive and well in this world.

So here's the big secret: Magic is the ability to manipulate natural energy, also known as bio-energy. Some of us are born with this ability, and others learn these as skills through quantum physics, meditations and prayer, occult study, and other numerous ways. We then travel through life on this earth, and those of us who believe in God, who is also Jesus the Christ, and the Holy Spirit, are magically blessed.

I remember exactly when I became aware of God. I was five years old, staring down into the little brook that ran through our yard, and suddenly had the feeling that someone greater than me was present and in charge. I knew that there was someone in the brook below, and that the same someone was in the meadow and the wind…that same someone was everywhere in the natural world. Someone made it and is in charge of it, and all of a sudden I just knew this.

It was around this time, too, that spiritual insights started coming to me. I would see spirits, tell my mother when a car was coming to the intersections, know who was coming to our home to visit, and generally refused to wear shoes. (Yes, this is a typical "witchy" personality trait.) One old man, a total stranger, even announced to my mother, "She is a witch," and nodded in my direction. I've never been quite sure if this was a cut down, a compliment, or a simple statement of fact.

My mother, being a liberated woman of the 1970's, took me to a "High Priestess" of Wicca that she knew for a ceremonial dedication, which was roughly half of the First Degree Initiation. So I was dedicated into the craft at the ripe old age of six. During my childhood, every chance I could, I was running around in the woods and wilds, knowing and learning natural magic and growing closer to God.

Now, for clarification regarding this deity of creation, I refer to God as a male, and will throughout this book in general. But specifically, I believe that the deity of God is male and female, and neither male nor female…but is one being that is largely beyond our understanding, with multi-faceted aspects and is mysterious in nature. God refers to self, as "I am that I am". The Holy Spirit (also called the Spirit, or the Spirit of Wisdom) is the female aspect of the divine God and represents the balance of the trinity: God the Father, God the Mother, and God the Son. Because of all these diverse aspects, and given the Jewish patriarchal society to which he came, Jesus makes God accessible to the human mind by referring to God in the male leadership divine: God the Father. Therefore, in this text and in worship, I will follow Jesus' example and refer to God in the aspect of "God the Father" and in the male gender.

At eleven, I was led by a sort of tugging sensation in my chest to believe that Jesus is the aspect of God that is a human being, and that he sacrificed his life here on earth to redeem my soul, and bridge the gap between God and humanity that was created by human sin (What I like to call: "self-will run amuck"). I accepted that right there in our local church that day. A few days later, I was baptized in the special tub, just behind the podium. I have done my best to follow Jesus ever since, even when it was sometimes hard and failure often ensued. And I always kept the magic, realizing that it is indeed, from God.

Jesus is the one who joins my being to that spirit of God in all living things for eternity, and I am profoundly grateful. I am a daughter of God; empowered with the Holy Spirit, a "Priestess" of Christ, a dedicated witch and a natural witch…exactly what He created and molded me to be. Thank you, God. Amen.

Jesus and Magic

So let's talk about our master, the redeemer of our souls, and God in the flesh here on earth: Jesus the Christ. As I write this, I'm trying hard to block out the memories of the fire and brimstone preachers of my past, which believed that their way of worshiping is the only way. They've done their damage through the ages, and I'm well aware of the burning times: when healers, witches, Wisemen and Wort-cunning Women were drowned, hanged and burned at the stakes. God bless them anyway. Now, I want to tell you about the Jesus that I know.

My Lord was foretold in every major religion of the ancient past…all those magical traditions of the Egyptian, Mesopotamian, Hebrew, Greek, Celtic and Zoasterian. These people were astrologers, magicians, healers, worshipers, wise men and women, and all believed that a "man-god" was not only viable, but was expected to appear (and/or reappear) and change mankind forever. The basic signs of the ancient prophecies regarding this "God-Man" are: a virgin birth, alignments and the appearance of new stars, to rise from the dead and live eternally after death, and the ability to perform supernatural feats.

Jesus fulfilled those prophecies and more. He healed a blind man by using the natural elements of dirt and spit (elemental potion.) Sorry, folks, check this out for your self in the Bible. He turned water into wine (alchemy, transmutation.) He prayed (talking and listening to God) in a garden...so hard that blood came from his skin (extreme concentration/meditation). He healed with a mere touch of his hand (manipulating bio-energy), instituted the regular act of eating and drinking in memory of Him (ritual worship), and physically rose from the dead after crucifixion (resurrection), glowing like a bright light (aura). Most magically of all, he accepted and transcended the evil of all our basic nastiness, allowing our souls to be forgiven and freed by the Creator. And did I mention that he did all this because he loves us perfectly? Astonishing.

Jesus followed a lunar calendar, told stories in allegory, and socialized with both Jews and non-Jews (the original pagans). He also hung out with both men and women (spiritual and social equality), and blessed those he came into contact with. But he didn't curse people, even when he got mad (and threw things.) This is my Jesus...the man who is also God. My brother and Lord. The man who performed real magic like the world had never seen before, and the Living God, whose spirit performs magic in and through us still. Great news is also afoot: He is coming to earth again in the flesh, as ruler and king. Yes, this is the Lord Jesus Christ that I know. And believing this makes me a Christian.

But being born with magical gifts also makes me a witch. Yep, I'd have been persecuted with two of my ancestors, and hanged with another, had I lived in the 17th century. The gifts of psychometry, discerning of spirits, bio-electric sensitivity and the ability to manipulate natural energy (living energy found in all God's creation, also known as the "breath of life") have all been labeled "witchcraft" by the established Christian religions, even though Jesus himself practiced such gifts. It's often been explained to me that when Jesus did it, it was not "magic", but "miracles" and "that is that!" Issue closed. For a Christian Witch, that's the same thing as saying, "tomato, tomaaaaato" and "because I said so." What? That just never worked for me.

But these types of linguistics separate us from the truth of Christ, the omniscience of God and the power of the Holy Spirit. It's just another way to feel spiritually superior to our fellow man. Quite frankly, I am not wise enough to judge another person's soul, are you? But I am wise enough to discern their spiritual motives and their closeness of relationship with the Lord by their actions and their aura. Well, most of the time anyway.

So for all you Christian Witches, hang in there. The Lord has not forsaken us, especially when we have a very personal connection through our relationship with Him. We will continue on doing his magical work through ritual, spells, potions and prayers. We will continue to worship our Almighty God. We will continue to evolve in our spiritual gifts and power of the Holy Spirit. You are not alone, even if you're the only Christian Witch you know. And really, there are a few Wiccans and even some Christians who truly love and even like us! So keep on blessing, encouraging, prophesying, healing, teaching, tending gardens, and divining spirits…this is how we know who we are: by our fruit!

Christian Witch's Creed

I believe in the one true God, who is God the Father (Creator of All), God the Son (The Messiah), and God the Holy Spirit (The Mother aspect of God, among us still).

I believe that Jesus the Christ is both God and the Son of God in manly flesh, who was born of a virgin, was crucified to wash away sin from my soul and died.

I believe that Jesus rose from the dead three days later and ascended into the heavens, from which he will return to earth again to pass judgement upon us all, both living and dead.

I believe that the Holy Spirit is within the believer and is the manifest spirit of God on and in creation. I believe the power of the Holy Spirit is manifest as magic, as demonstrated and promised by Lord Jesus the Christ, and is available to all believers in order to serve Him. As Christian Witches, it is our responsibility to use magic in His service to help others and ourselves. As God wills…so mote it be.

The Ten Commandments of God
You shall have no other gods before me.

You shall not make for yourself graven images and bow down and worship them nor serve them.

You shall not take the name of the Lord God in vain.

Remember the Sabbath day and keep it holy. You shall not work on the Sabbath day (the seventh day).

Honor your father and your mother.

You shall not murder.

You shall not commit adultery.

You shall not steal.

You shall not lie or bear false witness against your neighbor.

You shall not covet your neighbor's belongings, relationships or anything that is your neighbors.

The Christian Witch's Rede
Love thy God with all thy heart,
And Wisdom with the Spirit start.
Jesus Christ accept as Savior,
Strength and balance ever linger.
Keep the promise of eternal life,
Be the calm in worldly strife.
Harming none, give thyself to good,
Benevolence and joy to be understood.
Remember always the law of three,
What you put in, comes back to thee.
And listen well to other's being,
Quietly discerning what you're seeing.
Walk in beauty as the light,
Be not afraid of darkest night.
Humility guide thyself anew,
With faith in God be ever true.
In love and healing offer assistance,
But not against a wholesome resistance.
Never beg and never bend,
The words you offer to a friend.
Whenever ye are caught in hook,
To the Christ's commandments look.
"Vengence is mine," sayeth God,
Seek not revenge, lest evil trod.
Mind thy tongue, and guard thy mind,
Seek the truth, be ever kind.
Do this in the love of Christ, and God will keep you all of life.

What Christian Witchery is Not

It is appropriate here, to discuss the magical tenants of Christian Witchcraft from the negative perspective. I am very careful when meeting any kind of Witch, and especially another Christian Witch to discern their true spirit by what they believe and why they believe it. This takes time and the willingness to ask blatantly: "What do you believe about _____ (fill in the blank)?" and "Why do you believe that?" Discernment is necessary for appropriate action and reaction to people and situations...judgment is up to God. So instead of presuming to speak for all Christian Witches, I will proceed with what I personally proclaim.

I do not have "familiar spirits" that whisper evil suggestions in my ear or possess my body, other than the Holy Spirit of God as I understand that spirit, and guardian angels that are assigned to protect me. I do not worship Satan, or any angels, fallen or otherwise, nor do I attempt to boss them into doing my bidding. I do not worship God's creation, but wonder at it (all of it, even other worlds) and use it to enhance living. I, as a Christian Witch, do not "play God", but make every effort to be an instrument of His will. Nor do I believe that I may someday become God through any form of spiritual alchemy, church endorsed or other.

I do not believe in a god and a goddess, or any pantheon thereof, nor do I worship other creatures, such as sprites, fairies or sylphs. I do not call on spirits of the elemental quarters of the earthly watchtowers, nor fornicate with demons. I do not consult dead people for guidance, or use talking boards to open portals to the other worlds.

I do not draw upon evil energy from demons for control over my environment, practice The Great Rite, or any form of "sex magic" while worshiping a horny, drunken god in a great big orgy. I do not add blood to my prayers, or sacrifice goats on Halloween, nor do I vampirically suck bio-energy from other people for self-gratification.

I do not hypnotize, nor practice neuro-linguistic programming, or applied kinesiology on others to manipulate them into giving me what I think I may want, nor do I practice coercion. I do not curse milking cows, or send destructive storms to my wayward neighbors. And lastly, I do not steal babies in the night and boil them for "eternal youth" soap. I think that about covers it, and by the way, if you are thinking right now that these are amazing and ridiculous ideas, remember that these practices have existed and still exist in some occult theologies today.

Handling Criticism with Grace

There will come a time, if you tell people you are a Christian Witch, that you will be criticized. Christians will sometimes demand that their wives remove themselves immediately from your presence, and sometimes pray (right out in front of your home) that God saves your lost and sorry soul. Some Wiccans will even smile, pat you on the hand and decide that you're very cute, but sadly misguided or flat out demand that you "choose sides" and... they'll pray for you, too. The way to handle all these things is love, humor, and patience.

Thank the family members, friends and even those covert enemies for their prayers. Realize that they are often genuinely afraid of what they do not understand, and are not yet ready to accept any form of Christianity or Wicca other than their own as being a viable way of life. So stay calm, say a prayer, and keep on being who God made you to be. They'll come around, or be a very large pain in the butt, or both. But when you treat them with kindness, you please God. If they start making threats, however, (and yes, this does happen) call the police immediately.

When it comes to some of the Wiccans, remember that most of them have suffered persecution at the hands of other "well-meaning" or "just plain mean" Christians and often have very justified reasons for their venom and suspicions. Many of them also believe that the description of the word "witch" only means or is applied to the followers of the Wiccan faith, so they may think that you are somehow usurping their religion. Have patience with them, and explain that Wiccans aren't the only type of witches around. Be kind.

I was once even accused of "devil worshiping" by the mayor of a town I was living in…oh, the joys of a small town. But having conducted myself in a Christian manner, and having gained a good reputation as such, the mayor came to me personally and asked me to forgive her. I did. Remember that good and righteous actions often speak louder than name-calling.

Keep this in mind when a Wiccan starts "going off" on Christianity, they aren't usually attacking you personally, or even Jesus personally, they are just reacting to bad experiences. You don't have to jump in, teeth bared and defend the Lord. He is well able to defend himself. Instead share, laugh, forgive and maybe even cry together about your experiences and usually, they'll come to see who God made you to be, too.

The day after writing this, I awoke to the sounds of a preacher on the radio. My husband had "tuned in" for a little morning inspiration. So on comes the preaching about a wife who was both unfaithful, and hypocritical about it, taking her alms to the temple for a little "beforehand" forgiveness, and the minute her husband was out of town, taking her lover to her bed. So on goes the preaching which ended up being a full-blown "woman bashing" session, complete with stating that the spirit of wisdom written about in the Bible is really male, specifically, Jesus.

Off I went on a pretty good tangent myself, considering I hadn't even had a full cup of coffee. Forget that this was a story about disloyalty and hypocrisy…no…this was, to this preacher, a story about how deceiving and conniving women really are. Forget that when wisdom is mentioned in the Bible, the writers always refer to this spirit as "her", "she", etc...(Except for Paul, who was using the term to *describe* Jesus.) This guy is obviously flexing his supposed "male dominance" and "spiritual superiority" from the pulpit. I bet he has a small penis! (That one I didn't say out loud, but I sure thought it.) No wonder there's a passive/aggression between the sexes in the churches today! I was on a pretty good rip.

Now, my husband is a few years older, and a lot of years wiser than I am...and poor man, all he was looking for was a little morning's inspiration. But being the wise man that he is, he also knows to leave me alone when I'm busy overreacting. He loves me, and is well acquainted with my moods and even my hormonal surges. I love him, too.

So I then proceed to the shower. Funny how God likes to grant an epiphany to me while I'm in there. Happens a lot. So I'm showering and all of a sudden, I realize I was just writing about peace, love and tolerance and how to handle criticism. Oh, yeah, God definitely has a sense of humor, using that preacher and a story about hypocrisy, nonetheless. Very clever. This is how I know God is listening and loves me as a daughter: By creative teaching. I told my husband about this and we laughed. He had that wise little twinkle in his eye that let me know that he knew this all along, and that he loves his very passionate wife.

So for the record: "Father, please bless that preacher and surround him with truly loving women. Please change his heart toward love and forgiveness of the women who have hurt him in his past. And God, thanks for the lesson in hypocrisy, and for my husband. I love you. Amen."

Worship

The "right" way to worship God is in spirit and in truth. To observe the "Lord's Supper", and to "Love the Lord thy God with all thy heart, with all thy soul, with all thy mind and with all thy strength." And to "Love thy neighbor as thyself." These are the commandments that Jesus put forth. He didn't say that we'll go to hell for offering up herbs to God, or for burning a candle in His honor, or offering a prayer for the dead. We are not condemned for having a personal or family alter dedicated to Him, or for making magical charms, oils, or brews that draw good, natural energy toward us, our friends and family, and our homes.

We do these things in the spirit of perfect love and perfect trust in the truth of Christ. We pray with our minds, bodies, and spirits when we cast our prayer/spells. These elements of prayer are powerful, when our whole being is aligned with the Holy Spirit and the will of God through Christ. This is our trinity: God, Jesus, and Holy Spirit, all coming together as one God, *the* God, shining bright in us. That's where the real magic happens, and creates the light that shines in the world *through* us. This is the power of our magic, which is the power of God's magic *in* us.

And we celebrate this magical God with holidays, rituals,

spells, and other "witchy" living. We assemble teas, oils, amulets, lotions, charms, books, jars, waxes, pillows, sachets, herbal smudges and numerous other items for the benefit of others and ourselves. And we share the magical power of our God that is in us, through the flowing of bio-energy through our hands into these objects, and even into each other, blessing such for God's purpose. Then it's up to God to make it happen. It's about His will, not ours. Even when we've done all of these things, if it's not God's will, our own desired outcome is just not going to happen. We accept this fact.

But when it is God's will, the fulfillment we feel is a deep joy that can never be replaced. God has used us, His servants, to do something good and wonderful in this world. There is no deeper satisfaction for the Christian Witch. So let's get to worshiping!

Baptism (Your Dedication to Christ)

Baptism in water has been hotly debated through the ages as a requirement for salvation of the soul. I choose not to debate this because I am not qualified to judge whether someone is going to heaven or not. Only Jesus is...but I am sure that baptism by water submersion is at least an important act of worship. That, and the fact that Jesus himself was baptized in the Jordan River by his cousin John (another interesting and in my opinion, magical person who is well worth learning about.)

Most of us, as Christians, have been baptized through some sort of washing in water to symbolically encourage and acknowledge the cleansing of our souls and often to make a public announcement that we believe that Jesus is God, and all that this entails. From that moment on, we will be following Jesus Christ. This is one of the most beautiful rituals of the Christian faith, and is well worth pursuing.

It was one of the most touching and important moments of

my life when my son announced to us that he wanted to be baptized as a follower and believer in Christ. My heart literally skipped a beat and my brain suddenly stopped. That's excitement! After regaining my composure, my husband and I started prodding answers out of him to find out exactly why he wanted to be baptized, and who he personally believes Jesus to be. His answers were heartfelt, intelligent and more than that, he was sincere.

So off we went to the local Christian Church, and a few days later, my husband and the preacher baptized my son in the name of God the Father, God the Son, and God the Holy Spirit. The sun was shining, and the waters of the Colorado River sparkled with those brilliant diamond lights. My son was submerged and rose out of that water as a new born/born again believer and follower of Jesus the Christ.

As I write this now…tears are falling softly down my cheeks. My heart is singing with a host of angels, and I know, no matter what, that God has claimed my son as His own. What could I ever want more than that?

Communion (The Lord's Supper)

Jesus told us of a ritual that we, as Christians, must perform in remembrance of Him. This ritual is now commonly called Communion, or the Lord's Supper. The night before Jesus was going to be killed on the cross in Jerusalem, he gathered his closest friends and followers for a last meal together. Jesus served them bread, telling them "This is my body, broken for you…" (We repeat this and eat the bread at this time.) Then Jesus served them wine and said, "This is my blood, shed for you…" (We repeat these words and drink the wine here.) Jesus then said, "Do this in remembrance of me…" And we do. We also add in the traditional "Lord's Prayer", as Jesus taught it, translated to whatever language we are speaking around the world. Some Christians only partake of this once a month, once a year, and some even once a day. The point of this ritual is to remember Jesus and what He did for us.

BUT…and this is really important…before we partake in this ritual, we make sure that we have a clean heart, and have forgiven others, as we have been forgiven by God through Christ. We make sure we are not guilty of hurting others by our actions, prayers or inactions and thoughts. If you don't have this spirit of forgiveness in your heart, then you need to make whatever "it" is right with yourself and/or others before you practice this ritual, and ask God to forgive your transgressions. Otherwise, you will be condemning yourself to lots of guilt and pain. So make sure!

The Lord's Prayer
Our Father, who art in Heaven, hallowed be thy name.
Thy Kingdom come, thy will be done, on earth as it is in heaven.
Give us this day our daily bread and forgive us our trespasses,
As we forgive those who trespass against us.
Lead us not into temptation, but deliver us from evil.
For thine is the kingdom, and the power, and the glory
Forever and ever. Amen.

Personal and Family Alters

There once was a time, way back in the first and second centuries, which people had personal and/or family alters dedicated to God. At these altars, offerings and prayers were made to honor God and to thank Him for his grace and blessings. This tradition is sometimes carried on by Christian Witches. This is only a tradition, and not a commandment, so it's not necessary, but I personally feel more focused and spiritually attuned when at the alter.

An alter can be any table, box, space on the floor, windowsill, or whatever feels right. Mine is a wooden box that I keep magical items and reference books in. Fill your alter with symbolism that is right for you and your personal relationship with God. Regularly upon my personal alter are: 3 candles (one for Christ and two for the criminals that hung on the crosses by Him), a statue of Jesus as described in the Bible during his return (to remind me of the eternal hope and faith in Him. No, I do not bow down and worship a statue, just in case you're wondering.) I also often include my personal inspirational cards (for daily overall guidance from God), a white taper candle for prayer and a bottle of herbs or salt. I keep this alter very private in a room that I often pray and hang out in.

Our family alter is similar, but is out in the heart of our home for everyone, and is decorated by the seasons of the Holidays. I use magical symbolism, or correspondences, to decorate what best represents the season. Please refer to the Charts and the Spells/Prayer magic sections for more information...we'll get to that soon...I promise. But first things first, so...

Holidays/Holy Days: The Wheel of the Year

Note: These dates are based on the timeline of the Northern Hemisphere. Please adjust accordingly if you are an "Aussie", or are living elsewhere in the Southern Hemisphere.

October 31st: All Hallow's Eve (Halloween)

This is the night of the turning of the year from life toward death. The changing of the seasons from warm and sunnier to cold and darker. The night when the veil between the heavens and the earth is the thinnest, and the spirits can easily cross over to earth, or from the earth into the heavens. This is the night that we light a candle for the loved ones who have died this year, remembering them in our prayers and our lives.

And it's a wonderful time for children and families to gather together, talk about the living and the dead, and bless each other with treats and ghost stories. Dress up to honor your favorite deceased character, or…if you're still in the broom closet (and even if you're not) it's always great fun to dress as the traditional 17th century American witch, complete with broom and hat! There's lots of fun in celebrating the passing of life on earth to life in heaven, and it's also a great time to share your faith in Christ with others.

In my family, we decorate our family alter with harvest offerings, time pieces, shells, and whatever else feels "right" to dedicate our upcoming year to God, and to thank Him for the passing year and people. I personally begin this on October the first. (Bad witch! But it's lots of fun!) We have lights, pumpkins, bowls with money, and maybe a fake crow or two. And, of course, there are the magical correspondences that enter into our worship this night.

The colors of the celebration are: Orange, Purple, Green and Silver.

The herbal energies are: Bay Leaf, Lavender, Mugwort, Nutmeg, Sage, Ginger, Garlic and Mandrake. This is a great opportunity for cauldron magic.

The stone energies are: Black Onyx, Bloodstone, Amethyst, Moonstone, and Opal.

To Do: Decorate family alter. Carve gourds and pumpkins. Prepare teas for the season. Get candy and bible tracts for the trick-or-treaters. Light the candle and pray for the dead. Dress up and have fun.

Prayer for the Dead
Father, I/We light this candle on this night,
To be a beacon burning bright.
To light the path for loved ones dead,
That they may see now what's ahead.
Please take them to the Paradise,
Where you dwell now, enfold them thrice.
And with your glory, bring them peace,
That they may rest with love and ease. Amen.

November 1 through 30th: Thanksgiving
This is the time of the year when the final harvest is over; the produce is canned or dried and ready to last us through the winter months. The earth has begun its slumber and is rejuvenating in the wee hours of the night, and the moon begins to cast blue shadows over sparkling snow. These are the days that we thank God for our bounty, both spiritual and physical. We thank him for our families, friends, gardens, trees and all the good things that sustain us. I make sachets and charms. The family alter displays photos, pilgrims, turkeys, candles, grains, straw and raffia…anything that symbolizes what we are most grateful for. This year, I'm going to include the jars of chemicals that I use for the hot tub spa…for which I am truly grateful.

On the full moon of November, my family has the American traditional Thanksgiving feast with turkey and all the fixing's. Then we have a bonfire out in the fire pit on the side patio. We throw herbs on the fire with the pleasant smoke sending our prayers to God, and we pray the Thanksgiving blessing.

Colors of the celebration are: Orange, Yellow, and Burgundy.

The herbal energies are: Grains, Ginger, Garlic and Dill.

The stone energies are: Carnelian, Citrine, Smoky Topaz and Garnet.

To do: Decorate the family alter. Make sachets and charms. Enjoy the family and friends.

Thanksgiving Blessing
Thank you, Lord, for bounty divine,
For friends and family that our lives twine.
Thank you, Lord, for food from the earth,
And for the seeds that promise birth.
Thank you, Lord, for harvest this year,
And thank you for holding us in your arms near. Amen.

Full moon of December through the full moon of January: Yuletide and Christmas

Almost everyone's favorite time of the year, Yuletide is the busiest and friendliest. People sing along with Christmas carols, decorate homes, trees and stores…its just, well, jolly. Like most of us, it's also my favorite holiday. Once, I decorated a total of 9 trees, one of them was 16 feet tall and three of the trees were in my home, and considerably smaller. Ah, the energy of youth. But even for me, that was maybe a little overboard.

This is the season of general goodwill…a magic in itself, candle magic, knot magic and the best of all reasons to celebrate: the birth of Jesus the Christ. Even though we know that historically, Jesus was probably born in the spring, and that by the night of the Wisemen's visit, he was probably a toddler, the midwinter's Zoasterian tradition still holds the magic of the virgin birth, and the hope and promise of eventual peace on earth. Christmas is the proverbial seed of the "first source" of creation. God with us in the physical sense, called Emanuel in Hebrew.

Our family celebrates Jesus' birth on December 25th with the reading of the Christmas story as told by Luke in the Bible. This story features angels, Wisemen, humble beginnings, a wicked king, a bunch of shepherds (yes, as in people who nurture sheep) and a wondrous star. Talk about an exciting adventure! We give gifts with a wonderful prayer and have a great feast. If our neighbors, or any friend can't be with family this day, we invite them on over to our house, too. By this time, we've sent the Christmas cards out with "the news" of the year and a blessing from our family. Not to get ahead of myself, but Christmas Day is just plain magical.

Our decorating process begins on the first day of December (again, bad witch! But I just can't help it.) Decorating at our place involves lots of greenery, lights, and our family tree. These traditions are handed down through my family from Finland, and we tend to follow the Scandinavian decorating theme throughout the house. We place the Crèche (manger scene) on the family alter, along with evergreens, mistletoe, holly, lights, candles and a star. It's beautiful to be reminded of the joy and peace that comes with believing in the eternal good that is possible. Even soldiers at war have laid down their arms on Christmas Day…a very special magic from God.

On the full moon of December, or as close to it as we can get, we light the bonfire, dedicating it to the eternal light of the world, who is Jesus Christ. We sing Christmas carols while we enjoy the cold air, and hot cider with cinnamon sticks. We pray for the prosperity of the family, the town, our country, and the Earth. This year, I'm inviting our new friends and our new neighbors. What a great way to get to know them better!

Colors of the celebration are: Red, Green, White and Gold.

The herbal energies are: Frankincense, Myrrh, Holly, Mistletoe, Pine, Cedar, Apple, Cinnamon, Oak, Chamomile and Sage.

The stone energies are: Clear Quartz Crystal, Emerald, Ruby and Sapphire.

This is a great time to gather green, red and white candles for candle magic with gifts.

To do: Decorate the family alter. Send the Christmas letter and cards. Decorate the home and tree. Gather the friends and family for celebrations and enjoy.

The Frankincense and Myrrh Blessing
(For the giving of gifts.)
Red, green and white candles now I/We light,
To give the blessings of the night,
That wise men came and sought Him out,
And found the babe so whispered about.
They brought Him frankincense and myrrh,
And honored Him with fancy fur.
So when we give these gifts of thine,
He smiles on us with light sublime.
As God wills…so mote it be.

February 2nd: Candle Mass

Candle Mass is about asking God proverbially and physically to bring back the light into our darkest days. It's about remembering that the sun is still shining, even when our spirit or our circumstances are cold, dark and grim. Underneath the cold earth, tiny seeds are awaiting the warmth of spring, quietly waiting to be born anew. Lighting the candles this night reminds us that the cold will only last a season and is necessary in the harmony of God's creation. This is the day of hope for the future, and faith in God's power. This is the day to ask God to bring back the sun into our lives.

Colors of the celebration are: Green, Yellow, White candles…and lots of them.

The herbal energies are: Cayenne, Sea Salt, and Nettle.

The stone energies are: Diamond, Ruby and Citrine.
This is a great time for candle magic.
To do: Decorate the families alter and home with candles, herbs and stones. Pray with the lighting of the candles.

The Prayer for Light
Father, now we come to thee,
Asking that you hear our plea.
Into the world, bring back the light,
And banish darkness to the night.
Bring to our lives thy birth of love,
And keep our names in your book above.
As God wills…so mote it be.

Full moon of March: Resurrection (Spring Equinox)
Ah, Spring! Our Lord is risen from the dead, having been encased in a tomb for three days. He arises and is seen by the women who love him. He's shining like the sun in a heavenly aura. The light has returned, and the world is coming alive, too. He brings the freshness and promise of life with him in flowers and buds, birds, bees and babies. This is a triumphant time of year, full of the female energies of living births. As the women waited, grieving at the tomb, so do we still wait, giving birth to new life, having shared the blessing of our bodies, with both man and then carrying child.

Having accomplished bringing spiritual and physical life anew into the world, our Lord then rises into the heavens, preparing for the time when He will return again, as conquering King. He sends to us the Holy Spirit, the spirit of wisdom. Interestingly, in Greek, wisdom is referred to as a female noun: Sophia, an archetypical salute to the female aspect of the divine and truth. This spirit of God is in us, giving birth to pure, and white magic to the believers.

The cycle is complete, and the allegory of the life, death, and rebirth is amazingly illustrated in nature. Women are honored during this season with carrying the flame of divine life and endurance, faith and love. Spring is how we see the very real breath of life begin anew in the world.

Symbols of the celebration are: Wreaths, Rabbits, Eggs, Flowers and Ribbons.

Colors of the celebration are: White, Yellow, Cream, Green and Silver.

The herbal energies are: Rosemary, Roses, Mint, Ylang Ylang, Lavender and Patchouli.

The stone energies are: Bloodstone, Clear Quartz Crystal, and Amethyst.

This is a great time for circle magic.

To do: Decorate the family alter. Read the story of the Resurrection of Christ from the Bible. Hold a bonfire with songs that celebrate the Resurrection, like: He is Lord, Gloria Patre, In the Garden, Ride, As the Deer.

Resurrection Blessing
The new life comes now, this is Spring,
The breath now comes to living things.
What was once buried in the earth,
Now comes forth from darkness to birth.
God above, and so below,
Blessed, bringing forth that which was sown.
Mighty circle now shines anew,
Watered with the morning dew.
The Lord has risen from the dead,
And blesses still, for what's ahead.
For He loves us like the Spring,
Refreshing us with living wing. Amen.

May the 1st: May Day/Beltane

May Day (also known as Beltane) is the celebration of the masculine divine, the Father, the Hunter/Provider, the male fertilizer of the fullness of spring, birth and summer. The phallic symbology of male strength, vigor, support and life giving energy is strong on this day…so let's hear it for our men, without whom our lives would be infinitely unbalanced and dull.

The best phallic symbols of nature are the trees, whose roots are connected deep in the earth, whose strength is everlasting, and whose branches shelter, support, and sing harmony in the wind. So tie ribbons around tree branches with prayers for the season, and thankfulness for the men in our lives. Tell your man, brothers and sons how much you love and appreciate them!

Colors of the celebration are: Blue, Red and White.

The herbal energies are: Saw Palmetto, Horney Goat Weed and Wild Yam.

The stone energies are: Tiger's Eye, Ruby, and Black Onyx.

To do: Decorate the family alter. Tie the ribbons to the trees with prayer. Hold a bonfire and "cook-out" to honor the primal men in your life.

Blessing of the Trees
God, bless these trees and that they represent,
The strength of life, your breath you sent,
To the man and woman and child,
May you keep our spirits, like these trees…wild. Amen.

Full moon of June: Midsummer's (Summer Solstice)

Another of my personal favorite times of the year! The herbs are now flourishing, the trees are in full lush, and the roses are really growing with new leaves and gorgeous blooms. Our porch sparrows are fostering their first flock of the year out into the world, and the bees are busy pollinating and creating their ever-loved honey. The earth is at its most vigorous with life and having a generally good time. Living energy is pumping through everything! Midsummer is when God is smiling.

This is the greatest time of year for protection magic…blessing and protecting your home, friends, family, enemies (yes, enemies, too), gardens and everything! The magic is highest this time of year, so use it wisely to improve the lives of all.

This is also the perfect time to discover and contemplate the mysterious web of life. God works in patterns, and the spider's web is a perfect example of the interconnectedness, beauty and usefulness of those patterns. The same design is repeated in the night of endless stars, the elegance of a snowflake, the brain pattern of rhyboplasts, the matrix of a gem, and even down to the cellular level of all organisms. Admit it, you thought that the spider's webs were only good for scaring children at Halloween!

Yes, we are all very connected in God's creation, and what we do affects the balance that He has set. Be careful not to try and flow against God's patterns when working with His magic. To go against God's will is to go against God, and it will return to you threefold if you try.

Colors of the celebration are: Purple and Green.

The herbal energies are: Lavender, Calendula, Daisy and Mugwort.

The stone energies are: Amethyst, Malachite, and Lapis Lazuli.

To do: Decorate the family alter. Protection magics. Bonfire and prayers for protection and blessings. Spend time with family and friends for the night of festivities.

Binding Magic in God
Father, in this magic night,
With Holy Spirit burning bright,
Bless my/our magic, this your will,
And bring fruition to magic still.
Protect and bless these lives you make,
And love and joy, please do create.
Walk with me/us this night divine,
My/Our will is yours to ever bind. Amen.

Beginning the full moon of August through the full moon of September: Llamas (Beginning of Harvest)
Time to start enjoying the work you have put into your life this year...and begin stocking up for the winter months. The season to begin herbal harvesting and drying, your herbs should be ready in about a month to store up for the future, if you bundle and hang them. The gourds, fruits and vegetables are ripe, and if you have peppers...wow, at this point do you ever have peppers! This is the season of hard work, sharing and preparation for the future.

In our neighborhood, harvest can be kind of a group effort. We often go around to neighbors and help them harvest for some of the fruit, nuts, whatever, and we also trade our herbs for other items grown around the neighborhood.

True story: Our best neighbors and friends offered us pomegranates if we would just go and get them. So, of course, we headed down there one morning, and poof, we ended up clearing the pomegranate tree, pruning and laughing while we worked. This led to relocating their rather large weeping willow into our yard. We also transplanted herbal slips from our garden to theirs, and then my husband helped them repair their driveway! Thank you to our beloved friends, and to my husband, who did most of the tree relocation work. And by the way, my husband told our neighbors that next time they planned on chopping down a tree...don't tell his wife about it. Yes, I am one of those crazy tree huggers, with a special "soft spot" for willow!

So enjoy the work among friends, and celebrate the bountiful fruits of God this season. Decorate the alter with the "first fruits" available and dedicate them to God, thanking him for bounty, the ability to work, harvest and save.

Colors of the celebration are: Yellow, Green, Red, Blue and White.

The herbal energies are: Basil, Rosemary, Thyme and Mints.

The stone energies are: Emerald, Crysocolla, and Jasper.

To do: Decorate the family alter. Harvest and prepare for winter. Pray for forgiveness and make amends where necessary. Help your friends and neighbors harvest and prepare for the long winter months. Plant garlic now for the following summer harvest.

Prayer for the Preparation for Winter
Life has come now, to fruition,
Finding harvest and intuition.
Let us stock the bounty fine,
And honor God, who is divine. Amen.

These are the celebrations of us, in perfect love and perfect trust. From death and final harvest to the dormant seeds of life and light, toward the beginnings of new life, on through the fullness of life, and the first harvest to death again. Christian Witches, as is our nature, are connected to both God and earth, and are refreshed each year. As God wills...so mote it be.

The Lunar Calendar

The Jews, who are the first people to whom God began to fully reveal himself, were given an understanding of time that revolves around the moon. Jesus, who was born into this world as a human, and a Jew, also followed a lunar calendar.

When the Romans came to power, they followed a solar calendar. Julius Caesar then implemented the "Julian" calendar (also solar), which was then replaced by the most used calendar of today, the "Gregorian" calendar. So, because Jesus followed the lunar cycles, (and not Caesar's) these are the times that I personally believe God has established for us. The lunar phases are the natural phases of magical energy that Christian Witches most often identify with.

Humanly, the science of astronomy has proven that the magnetic field of the moon affects the earth, including the rise and fall of the waves in the ocean. We would be foolish to believe that the waves are the only thing affected by lunar energy. Even seasoned farmers and ranchers plant and harvest by moon cycles. So, in the spirit of God, whose energy permeates the moon and stars, magical energy is formed, and that energy is accessible for those of us who dare to use it for God's will.

The new moon is when the moon is totally shadowed from the sun by the earth and is not visible. This is the time of the lunar month when hopeful and waiting energies are high, and is a great time for spells involving these. The waxing moon is the phase in which the moon begins to grow toward fullness, prosperity and growth energies are high, and is a great time for these types of spells. The full moon is the time of each month when the energies of God's magic are highest, and is also when the Jews begin their festivals. This is the best time for the most powerful ritual and any spell/prayers of God's magic. The waxing moon is when the moon begins to fade back down, and is the best time for the binding and banishing of the negative influences and energies in our lives.

There are thirteen moons per year, from new moon to new

moon, beginning with the new moon in January of the solar year. Have you heard of the "blue moon"? That's when there are two full moons during a solar month, and is a good time for love spells. There are also the eclipses, which in Jewish terms are times of change. These eclipses have both lunar and solar energies to work with, and are wonderful for transformations, pure joy, and balance in worship and magic.

Bubble, Bubble, Toil and Trouble...(Shakespeare)
The "Crafting" of Prayers

Praying Spells/Casting Prayers

Spells are prayers with elements of representation and offering. I often refer to this as "Praying a Spell", "Spell/Prayers", "Prayer/Spells", "Spells", or "Casting a Prayer" and use these terms interchangeably. The elements that I am referring to are: raising energy from God's created elements of earth, fire, water, air and spirit, expending energy, absorbing energy from natural sources, and sending these energies through prayer to God to petition His will in the results. I utilize herbs, strings, crystals, jars, candles, just about anything that focuses these positive energies and my concentration for the best results. To do this, it is necessary to have a basic knowledge of signature doctrine and symbolic representations. This is known as sympathetic magic. So here we go...

The Doctrine of Signatures is the belief that God has marked all natural things with a sign of correlation to other things that are mutually beneficial, or other aspects that cancel each other out and balance the bio-energy. For example: In the 16th century, the walnut was often used to treat brain disorders because the walnut resembles (or "signatures") the brain closely, with its hard outer shell and inner "wrinkly" nuts in pairs. It looks like a brain; therefore, God tells us that it is "brain" food. Interestingly enough, we now know that the walnut is high in good fats that actually do "feed" our brain, and help our thinking processes. But, if your problem was thinking too much, and being out of touch with your emotions (i.e. Mania) by the Doctrine of Signatures, the heart-shaped Catnip leaf would be appropriate. And again, it is now proven the Catnip is an effective and mild sedative for humans…but not for cats. So observe closely. God is indeed "signing" his creations, we just need to study and notice.

Sympathetic Magic is about symbolic representation. In other words, "this represents that". For example: "This blue candle represents the healing that God can bring to my Friend." "This golden ribbon represents our spiritual connection to God." "This burning of sage represents the cleansing of my aura or a space." "The smoke from this rosemary represents my love rising toward heaven." "This cauldron represents the birth-giving process for this blessing." You get the idea…

The symbolic representation is based again on similarities, and these representations should mean something to you personally. The more personal to you, the more powerful the energies, the more powerful the focus and the concentration will be that is required for this type of prayer. These representations can be colors, herbs, elements (fire, earth, air, water), subtle energies (auras), stones, days of the week, stations of the moon, a specific time of day, or other correlations that mean something to you. There are many charts of correlations that have proven effective in petitioning prayers through sympathetic magic. Please refer to these charts when crafting your own magic.

Casting Circles...Sacred Space

Once you start praying in very powerful ways, strongly connecting to the creative power of God, then the other beings and spirits of the universe will become interested in you. Your aura will start shining with shakina glory and the others, both good and evil, will take notice; especially during your actual spell casting. In order to protect against attack from malevolent spirits, human or otherwise, it is wise to raise a magical circle of energy around you, creating a sacred space that only good can appreciate.

There are many ways of "casting circles", but these are my personal best, based on experience and having tried other techniques. First, I visually and physically "pull" energy with my mind from the earth, and let that energy gather around my body. When I feel the energy begin to lift the hair on my arms, I then mentally "push" it into a sphere around me and feel God's protection of the sphere, with me inside it. This creates a very bright, white light around my aura. I then check the sphere for any ripples, hooks, tears, or black or gray areas and "smooth" them with the light energy in the sphere until they are clear and repaired. To release this circle after the prayer is done, I "unwind" it back into the earth, letting the energy absorb softly.

For emergencies, when I'm feeling emotionally or spiritually attacked, I quickly "pull" up a sphere of visualized and strong ivy vines, then wind and weave them until they create a thick sheet of green between me and the attacker. I then move away from the person and make a mental statement of blessing. This technique is only for spiritual and mental attacks. If someone attacks you physically...kick their (beep)...and/or get away. Survive the situation however you need to.

After removing myself from that situation and letting the vines return to the ground, I mentally ask God to grow the attacker in His will, and bless them with the Holy Spirit. This is turning the other cheek, although I don't continue to expose myself to the attacker unless they change, and sometimes they do.

The third circle that I use for the most intense of meditative prayers is the circle of candles. Using the concept of the five elements, I place the candles around me in the positions of the Morning Star, which announced the birth of Jesus Christ. The connotation here is the connection to God in heaven, not what is known as "high or ceremonial magic", which I personally do not practice because it involves calling on "other" spirits. For more information about this type of magic, there are lots of sources out there. Please use spiritual discernment when exploring these. So, back from the tangent then…Starting at the north, I light the candles with the following prayer, beginning with the candle to the right and lighting in a clockwise fashion (called doesil).

To create the circle:
I call upon God, Creator of Air,
Be with me now and give me care. (Light first candle.)
I call upon God, Creator of Earth,
Who comes and gives the living birth. (Light second candle.)
I call upon God, Creator of Water,
Within this circle, bring your power. (Light the third candle.)
I call upon God, Creator of fire,
Fill me with your living pyre. (Light the fourth candle.)
I call upon God, Creator of Spirit,
Complete the circle, enjoin within it. (Light the fifth candle.)
God is Alpha, the circle is whole.
God is Omega, and in control.

To release the circle:
(Blow out the candles in the reverse of which you lighted them, called moving "Widdershins" or counter-clockwise.)
God is Alpha, the circle now released.
God is Omega, may He be pleased.

"Cleansing" and "Charging" Items for Prayer/Spell Purposes
Objects "remember" energy that has touched it, whether it's very subtle or extreme. For instance, if a tree is struck by lightening, it often splits from the sudden impact of energy. People, too, have a measurable energy field emanating from our bodies, all the way down to the cellular level. That energy field also affects the cells and molecules of other objects, although we don't often emit enough energy to blow trees apart. And even if you can do this, you shouldn't!

Our energy is much more subtle, but still affects objects around us by leaving a readable "imprint". Some of the best conductors and collectors of this type of energy are crystals and metals. That is why crystals are used in laser and computer technologies, and metal is used as electrical wiring. So, to tell if an object is negatively charged, feel it. Touch it and really pay attention to what comes to mind. Note any images, sounds and emotions that you feel when touching the object. If it is a good feeling, then it has positive energy. If it's a bad or strange feeling, it has negative energy.

This is how the gift of psychometry works. It's a form of discerning energy, also known as discerning spirits. People who can sense these energies naturally are often called "witches", "sensitive", or "psychics." If an object has been affected by strong negative (traumatic) energy, the object remembers the trauma, and will also conduct all the matching trauma energy around it. This is often what it means when someone says an object is "cursed." So, we need to "cleanse" this negative energy from the object to help us pray for positive results. If you're unsure about any item, then cleanse it.

To cleanse an object of negative energy, I recommend washing it in salt water if it's small, and smudging with sage, leaving it in the rain and the sun if it's large. Smudging with sage is done by burning sage leaves and passing the object through the smoke, or letting the smoke drift around the object. This may take a few times before the negative energy is gone, depending on the strength of the energy and how good a conductor the item is. Just feel the object, and if it still makes you feel uneasy, cleanse it again until it feels right and good.

To charge an object with your energy, touch it, hold it, put your hands on it and gently "push" your natural energy field onto it. When done properly, your hands will feel warm in the palms and this often takes some practice. Then visualize happy memories, and feel the emotions of happiness and love. "Push" those wonderful emotions through your hands and into the object. Ta Da! The object is now positively charged with your good energy. This also helps in healing and is known in Christian circles as the "laying on of hands." Just be *very* careful about who "lays hands" on you!

Tools of the Craft

To work the crafting of magical prayer, there are a variety of tools that are useful. These listed here are traditional craft tools that are both fun and easy to use. They are "practically" functional and are also used as tools for focusing your concentration and energies. Some witches dedicate these tools to magical use only, but others, like me, use some of them for both magic and the mundane. For example, my mortar and pestle are so heavy that they also make an excellent paperweight when I'm writing. Tee, hee, hee!

The Book of Shadows is the book that a witch uses to keep all the hidden knowledge that they have collected and compiled over the years. It's called a book of Shadows because the secrets it contains are often considered to be hidden (Occult) or "in the shadows". This book is extremely personal and can range from a simple notebook to a leather bound and highly decorated tri-fold tome to a book of shadows in cyberspace. The choice is always yours. I even know a witch who uses a three-ring binder system.

Along with this vital magical information, I also keep a copy of my spells, prayers, some art and poetry. My book has magical charms that dangle from built in ribbon bookmarks. I paint, stamp, paste and scrapbook inside this book and someday plan to pass it on to my loved ones as a family heirloom.

The broom, also called the besom, is used for sweeping bio-energy around a space, be it alters, a room, a home, a circle or a property. We sweep the energy towards and away, or gather it together to add extra energy to other items. If you so choose to use this tool, your broom should be very personal to you. My broom is made of cinnamon branches that are bound together to form a handle, and fanned freely at the bottom. In the bottom of the whisking, I have tied colored ribbons around herbs that are symbolic for me.

Other brooms I've seen are made of cornhusks, willow branches, pine needles and every combination of natural fibers you can think of. When buying or crafting your own broom, just make sure it carries the positive energies of God the Creator, and enjoy this quintessential "witch's" tool.

Among my collection is also a 12-inch, 3 footed cauldron of cast iron with a handle. This one is an antique that has spent time at a hearth, warming stews and boiling rags. I love the energy of this piece, and use it on my own kitchen hearth, which happens to be a modern electric stove. I love how it looks there, the old and the new, and always ready to brew. Please refer to the Cauldron Magic section for more information.

Mortar and Pestles are used for grinding herbs, crystals, salts and the like. If it needs ground with lots of personal energy, I use this tool when I want to add a little extra magical "oomph" to a spell or recipe. Otherwise, I generally use the modern equivalent: my electric coffee grinder. The choice is always yours.

Magic wands are used to specifically pull, point and direct energy and can be used in conjunction with casting prayer/spells. These can be as simple as a pine stick, or as complex as a cast metal with a crystal tip. My favorite wand is made of weeping willow, and has a woven, braided handle made of ribbons with dove feathers attached in the hanging tassel. I have also found crystal "wands" useful in manipulating healing energies in and around the body.

Collections of herbs, candles, colored strings or ribbons, crystals, jewelry, gardens (flowers, herbs, vegetable and fruit), and other personal collections are useful in healing, praying and any act of worship. Be creative and enjoy discovering your own personal tools.

The Wisdom of the Mage: A Formula for Magic

Magically powered prayer can also have a formula. Most witches use the outline of the formula called The Wisdom of the Mage. And it goes like this: "To Know, To Will, To Dare, To Remain Silent." This helps keep our own ego out of the spells, and keeps us from bragging on ourselves. It keeps us in humility, which is knowing your place in God's world. The following is my usual prayer/spell formula for sympathetic magic. It's kind of like a church or prayer "liturgy." Should you choose to use a formula for casting prayers, make sure it is one with which you are personally comfortable.

My Basic Formula for Casting a Prayer/Spell

1. Determine what I'm praying: Asking for something, sending praise, sending thanks, just spending time with God and connecting, etc...
2. Consider if this prayer/spell is truly in God's will. Does this honor the commandments of Jesus? If not, leave it alone. (To Know.)
3. Ask the Holy Spirit to empower me in this endeavor, giving blessing to the prayer/spell.
4. Gather the items and correspondents that represent the important parts of the prayer.
5. Charge the items by adding my energy to them, or to the energy that the item may contain itself. (To Will.)
6. Writing the prayer that gives words to the meaning of the items.
7. Casting of the protective circle.
8. Adding the items with the prayers to perform the spell. (To Dare.)
9. Binding the spell in God's will and accepting the outcome, even if it's not what I personally wanted. As God wills...so mote it be!
10. Thank God for loving me, through Jesus Christ the Lord.
11. Release the circle.
12. Clean up, and dispose of the items or keep them...whichever seems right.

Tell no one of specifically whom it was cast for, or upon. Only tell others the outcome in praise of God, be it what I personally wanted or not. Keep other's confidentiality, never gossip or brag about a spell. (To Remain Silent.)

Prayer/Spells

Please know that all prayer/spells, charms, and recipes are

somewhat interrelated in the methodology, and always: The best prayer/spells, charms, and recipes are the ones you make yourself, with your energy mixing with God and His creation. So here are two of my favorite prayer/spells to help you get started.

True Love Spell
Ingredients: Mortar and Pestle. 1/2 Teaspoon each: Chamomile, Catnip, Clove, Lavender, Cinnamon, Basil, Roses, Dill, Peppermint, Rosemary, Thyme, Ginger, and Flaxseed.
To Do: Gather ingredients and cast a circle. Speak aloud while grinding into powder, and add appropriately while you pray:
Beginning with roses, I ask God for true love,
Then stir in the chamomile for peace of the dove.
Clove represents the heat of the sun,
Catnip is added to stir in the fun.
Now comes the cinnamon to turn up the spice,
And thyme for the seasons, the energy's nice.
Protection from basil and then dill to guard,
The ginger for health, and strength by the yard.
Flax, you'll see deeply, and peppermint clear,
The passion that ebbs and flows through the years.
Harmony from lavender, the joy never ends,
Sealed now with rosemary, the attraction begins.
I blend this together to powder so fine,
May my true love be revealed in time.
Now sprinkled around, I am patient and free,
As God wills…so mote it be!
(Release the circle and thank God for his love and grace.)

To Break a Curse on Home and Family
Ingredients: Sage smudge stick (can be purchased at most herbal

stores), Broom (also called a Besom), Olive Oil for anointing, White candles and energetic music. 1 Teaspoon each: Horseradish, Clove, Sage, Olive Leaf, Mandrake, Garlic, Rosemary, Juniper Berry, Bay Leaf, Mugwort, Salt and Blessed Thistle.

To Do: Take a ritual bath and visualize yourself bathing in white light from heaven, then anoint your body with olive oil by "drawing" a cross on your forehead and hands. Light a candle in every room and open one door. Begin burning the sage and "sweeping" the energy with the broom in the areas farthest away from the door, praying as you go around the home:

Break this hex, oh Lord, I pray,
Make us safe by night and day.
Bless the one who sent the curse,
And make the damage now reverse!

Sweep every room in the home, chasing the negative energy curse out the open door. Close the door and begin anointing all the thresholds and windows with the oil, making the shape of the cross while praying:

With this oil, I now bind, Loving of the Godly kind,
Sealing peace around about, and keeping nasty sorcery out!

Grind the herbs together and pour lines of the powder across the gates in the yard, garden, and the outside of the baseboards while praying:

As God wills…so mote it be!

Potions

Teas

The most popular form of potions are now called "Herbal Teas." In centuries past, herbs were used to heal, bless, and worship by priests, witches, soldiers, royalty, peasants, scholars, farmers, and everyone else on the planet earth. It is my personal belief that God created plants as the primary nourishment and for the healing of our bodies. The Bible even refers to "bitter herbs" being healing and good for us. Almost all diseases are curable by plants or plant derivatives.

Choose your herbs wisely, and grow your own organically if you can. If not, try and order herbs that are organic, and have good color, smell and texture. Study these plants and their uses, both medicinal and magical. Get to know which are poisonous, and which are not and how to handle them. There are lots of resources to learn from, and most of all: Visit your neighborhood herbalist or the white witch with the herb garden (often known as a "Hedge Witch") down the street! Build a relationship with these people because their knowledge is invaluable.

To make a very strong, healing tea, use fresh herbs if you can…wrap them in a cotton/muslin bag, or a traditional tea steeper and soak one or two teaspoons of herbs in 2 cups hot water. If using dried herbs, use 1 teaspoon per cup of hot water. Following are some herbal recipes for common ailments, with portions listed in the alchemical tradition of "parts". For example: 1 Garlic would equal 1 (whatever unit of measurement you are using: teaspoon, drops, cups, etc…depending on how much you want to make.) Just keep the parts the same measurement choice, and you should be fine.

As with all herbal supplements, consult your health care practitioner, especially if you are pregnant, nursing, have allergies to any herbs or are taking prescription medications. And by the way, most of these taste pretty awful, but they work for me, most of my friends, and my family. Add honey, real maple syrup or stevia if you need it sweetened.

Cold/Flu Tea
1 Echinacea
1/8 Siberian Ginseng
1/8 Dandelion Root
1/2 Garlic
Steep in 2 cups hot water for about 11 minutes.

Headache Tea
1 Ginkgo Biloba
½ Peppermint
½ Ginger Root
½ Passionflower
Steep in 1 cup hot water for about 12 minutes.

Heartburn Tea
1 Ginger
¼ Licorice
Steep in hot water for about 5 minutes.

Allergies/Hay Fever Tea
1 Stinging Nettle (dried herb only)
½ Garlic
½ Dandelion Root
Steep in 1cup hot water for about 13 minutes.

Stress Reliever Tea
1 Catnip
1 Passionflower
½ Dandelion Root
Steep in 1cup hot water for about 11 minutes.

Painkiller Tea
Do not use if taking blood-thinners.
3 White Willow Bark
1 Chamomile
1 Ginger
Pinch of Cayenne if desired.
Steep in 1cup hot water for about 11 minutes.

Detox Tea
3 Red Clover
2 Dandelion Root
1 Horseradish Root
1 Stinging Nettle (dried herb only)
Steep in 2 cups hot water for about 17 minutes.

Sleeping Tea
3 Chamomile
1 Hops
1 Catnip
1 Valerian
Steep in 1 cup hot water for about 7 minutes.

Tinctures

Another popular form of potion is the "Herbal Tincture". Tinctures are an extraction of the energy and chemicals of a plant by alcohol or apple cider vinegar. The alcohol extracts more of the useful chemicals of the plant and faster than the vinegar, so I use 80 proof vodka to make mine.

Tinctures are very easy to make, but are also time consuming. Take a pint jar with a wide-mouth and fill it half full of the herb or herbs you have chosen. Powder form is best. Fill the jar to the top with the vodka or apple cider vinegar. Put the lid on and let the herbs soak in the vodka for one lunar month (about 29 days.) Make sure you shake the jar at least once a week. When the time is complete, strain the herbs out of the liquid with an unbleached cotton cloth or unbleached coffee filter and you have a very strong tincture. If you leave the tincture at full strength, you can add a few drops to apple juice, water, tea, soup, or use directly if you can.

My most popular tincture is called the Viral Infection Tincture. People have used this for colds and flu, sinusitis, and to boost their immune systems.

Viral Infection Tincture
In a pint jar, mix the following herbs:
¼ Cup Ginger Root Powder
¼ Cup Garlic Powder
¼ Cup Horseradish Root Powder
1/8 Cup Cayenne Pepper (90 BTU)

Fill jar to the top with vodka and let set 1 lunar month. Shake at least once a week. When the month is complete, strain the powder from the liquid. Add 1 pint of Apple Cider Vinegar and mix. Bottle in 2 - 1 pint jars and store in a cool, dark place.

Oils

Which brings us to the potion form called "Oils." Use of oils dates back thousands of years into the religious texts of the Mesopotamian regions. Jesus was even anointed with scented oil by a woman before his death. This oil was probably spikenard, as it was poured upon his head from an alabaster jar. Though very expensive, spikenard is still used today in religious services.

Oils are most often used as aromatherapy today, and this "therapy of scents" utilizes essential oils for help in healing. Scent plays an important role in how we experience God's world, and affects our moods through memory and also by stimulating the production of hormones in our brain and body. When you feel good, healing takes place. By using these essential oils, we are basically using the essence of the energy and scent of each plant.

Essential oils are pure oils from plants that have been extracted by a hot or cold steam diffusion process. This process requires specialized equipment. Therefore, I choose to buy my essential oils from manufacturers or herbal retail stores. For the best results, try to get oils that are labeled "therapeutic grade." I add these to unscented lotion base, soap base, bath salts and other "carrier oils" like safflower, grape seed, or almond.

Aromatherapy can be administered via massage, added to a bath, smelling from tissues or from the bottle, and my favorite technique: the oil burner method. Oil burners are sold at most health food stores and are often shaped like a tea light candle holder, with some sort of bowl on the top that will contain the oils. By warming the oils with the tea light underneath, the aromas are released into the air. This process usually lasts about two hours. After the candle has extinguished, the oil should be replaced. Here are a few recipes to try:

General Stress
1 Tablespoon Carrier Oil
11 Drops Lavender Oil
11 Drops Rosemary Oil

Headache
1 Tablespoon Carrier Oil
13 Drops Lavender Oil
9 Drops Peppermint Oil

Energy
1 Tablespoon Carrier Oil
10 Drops Clove Oil
6 Drops Lemon Oil
10 Drops Orange Oil

Common Cold
1 Tablespoon Carrier Oil
4 Drops Tea Tree Oil
6 Drops Rosemary Oil
3 Drops Peppermint Oil

Menstrual Cramps
1 Tablespoon Carrier Oil
10 Drops Geranium Oil
8 Drops Grapefruit Oil
6 Drops Lavender Oil

Powders

Magical herbal powders are useful to create because they store well, can be sprinkled around a room, in bedding or a bath, and can be added easily to drinks and food, or even burned in a censor, or added to cauldrons. Tossing a very small amount into a fire, just a pinch, can flare up into wonderful colors, depending upon the herbs used. You can add magical powders to dream pillows, stuffed animals, or in a little sachet for your pocket. One of my favorite ways is to use a mixture of herbal powders that I call "Hedge Powder" to create a barrier at doors and windows to keep evil spirits from entering our home or space.

I've even used powders as a "snuff" for health remedies! As always, be careful about what herbs you use in your powders, as some herbs are poisonous. Consult an herb book if there's any question as to toxicity.

Grinding dried herbs is easy, and yes, they must be dry herbs to make powders. I use my little stainless steel, electric coffee grinder and it works magnificently. But if I'm feeling particularly "witchy", I use my old mortar and pestle to grind the powder down. When I do this, I always grind in a clockwise motion (doesil) to infuse more positive energy into the mix. With powders, there are a lot of options.

The following recipes are for magical use only and should not be ingested. Again, I used the alchemical ratios for measurements of your choice. These recipes are designed as focus tools to help you concentrate on God's will in a suitable situation.

Banish Powder
6 Garlic
1 Stinging Nettle (dried herb only)
3 Ginger Root
1 Poke Root
3 Horseradish Root
3 Bloodroot

Prayer Powder
6 Ginger Root
3 Spearmint
3 Lavender
3 Passionflower
3 Rose Hips
3 White Willow Bark

Dream Powder
6 Lavender
1 Lemon balm
3 Damiana
3 Peppermint
1 Passionflower

Peace Powder
6 Damiana
3 Comfrey
3 Chamomile
3 Lavender

Love Powder
6 Roses
3 Wild Yam Root
3 Damiana
3 Horney Goat Weed
1 Rosemary
3 Passionflower

Positive Energy Powder
6 Ginseng
6 Goto Kola
6 Echinacea

Prosperity Powder
1 Angelica Root
6 Flax Seed
3 Damiana
6 Cinnamon
3 Fennel Seed
1 Goldenseal

Charms

A charm is an item that is infused with the personal energy from the prayer/spell that is cast, and also serves as a reminder of that prayer. A reminder, if you will, with a little bit of energy of its own. These include sachets or prayer bags, jewelry, cauldron, broom, basically anything can be "charmed" and dedicated to a specific magical purpose. Please refer to the "cleansing and charging" sections for reference.

But most often, a charm is made for a specific purpose by creating something with magically infused items; and created by the process of a prayer/spell, using sympathetic magic. Here are some of my favorites, so get creative and enjoy!

Triquetra Joy Charm
Ingredients: 3 Sunflower Seeds, 3 Rose Hips, 1 Small bag painted with a sun of 9 rays, 3 feet of yellow ribbon, 3 drops Orange Oil, 3 teaspoons of Lavender Flowers, and 1 small, clear quartz crystal.

To Do: Gather the ingredients and make sure all items have no negative energy attached to them. Cleanse your mind of all negative thoughts. Follow this prayer, adding the items as you pray:

Into this sunny bag of rays,
Add sunflower seeds and oil of orange for happy days,
Then add to rose hips for loving ways.
On then, to lavender for kindly peace,
And adding quartz, the magic to increase,
Knot the ribbon thrice with prayer, then cease.
(Prayer for each knot.)
God of life, please send to me,
The powers of joy and harmony.
Send me joy and peacefulness,
Teach me to live in happy bliss.
(Tie the bag closed with the knotted ribbon.)
Release the circle and happiness I'll see,
That joy will come in blessings three,
As God wills…so mote it be!

Release the circle and keep this charm in a well-lit area of your home, office or other living space.

Charmed Family Gravy
Ingredients: Pot or pan, little bits of the meat that you're serving, 1 box or can of broth, wheat flour, 1 teaspoon salt, 1 teaspoon pepper, 1 teaspoon rosemary.

To Do: In the pot, add the meat and broth and bring to a medium heat. Stir in wheat flour to a gravy consistency while stirring doesil.

Add the salt and pray: God of all, please cleanse our minds of past nastiness and hurt feelings this holiday.

Add the pepper and pray: God of all, please add interest to our conversations this holiday.

Add the rosemary and pray: God of all, please add love over all things to one another this holiday.

Keep stirring while praying:
Father, spin this rosemary 'round,
To bring us only loving sound.
Laughter, joy, surround us thrice,
Make our words be only nice.
As God wills...so mote it be.

The first time I made this, our guests behaved wonderfully, and I got so many compliments on the gravy that it is now requested for all our feasts. So serve this to family and friends and enjoy!

Charts

Element Chart

Air: Air is the element that carries sound, sunlight, knowing, and information. This is the element that connects with: To Know.

Fire: Fire is the element that burns with purity, passion, truth and cleansing. This is the element that connects with: To Will.

Earth: Earth is the element of nurturing, transition, grounding energy and energy stabilization. This is the element that connects with: To Dare.

Water: Water is the element of flowing energy, peacefulness, and other worlds. This is the element that connects with: To Remain Silent.

Spirit: Spirit is the element that is created by God to bind all energies together in balance and worship of Him. Spirit is the element that Jesus also healed (by healing the great divide caused by sin) while on the cross so that we can connect with God.

Herbal Energy Chart: Magic Only

List Compiled for magical purposes only. Do not eat without further study in medicinal herbalogy. **Some of these are toxic if ingested.**

Acia Berry: Cleansings and Inks/Dyes.
Acacia: Clairvoyance and Protection.
Acorn: Wisdom and Strength.
Allspice: Magical powers and family matters.
Almond: Anger management.
Angelica: Protection and Exorcism.
Apple: Love and Healing.
Apricot: Heals heartbreak.
Avocado: Female Fertility.
Baby's Breath: Love for children.
Bamboo: Extra blessing.
Barley: Harvest and Prosperity.
Basil: Love and Exorcism.
Bay Leaf: Clairvoyance and Healing.
Beans: Grounding energies with the earth.
Benzoin: Purification and Intellectual pursuit.
Bergamot: Prosperity.
Black Cohosh: Women's issues.
Blessed Thistle: Blessings and Banishing hatred and ill will.
Buckwheat: Grounding energies with the earth.
Butcher's Broom: Binding a spell and magic in general.
Calendula (Marigold): Prophetic dreams.
Carnation: Positive energy.
Catnip: Calming and Loving and Sex.
Cayenne: Cleansing and removing negativity.
Cedar: Anointing and Concentrating.
Chamomile: Nightmares and Meditation.
Cherry: Fertility.
Cinnamon: Healing and high-energy vibrations.
Clove: Stops gossip and negativity.
Clover: Extra blessings and Protection.
Comfrey: Protection and Healing.

Coriander: Love.
Corn: Prosperity.
Cotton: Spiritual growth.
Cucumber: Male fertility.
Daffodil: Safety at night.
Daisy: Managing depression.
Damiana: Women's issues.
Dandelion: Knowing.
Dill: Protection and love.
Dragon's Blood: Magical energy and purification.
Eucalyptus: Healing and Communication.
Fennel Seeds: Health and Wealth.
Fern: Love issues.
Flax Seeds: Knowing and Beauty.
Frankincense: Consecration and Exorcism.
Gardenia: Love and Passion.
Garlic: Protection, Cleansing, Binding and Exorcism.
Geranium: Healing.
Ginger: Passion.
Grape: Healing and Addictions.
Guto Kola: Remembering, Thanksgiving and Sentiments.
Hawthorne: Protection.
Hazel, Witch: Fertility, Beauty and Knowing.
Heather: Rain.
Hibiscus Flower: Knowing.
High John the Conqueror: Legal issues and warring.
Holly: Protection and Divinity.
Hops: Healing and Soothing.
Horehound: Death issues and Healing.
Horseradish: Health and Passion.
Ivy: Guarding and Protection.
Jasmine: Wild Love and Heartbreaks.

Lavender: Peace, Love, Healing and Tranquility.
Lemon: Friendships.
Lemon Balm: Success.
Lettuce: Resting and Cleansing.
Lily: Peace and Fertility.
Magnolia: Happiness and Heartbreaks.
Marsh Mallow: Increase.
Mandrake: Binding for all spell/prayers.
Maple: Changes and Transformations.
Mesquite: Cleansing and Binding.
Mints: Healing and attracting positive energy.
Mistletoe: Love and Hunting success.
Mugwort: Binding spell/prayers.
Myrrh: Blessings.
Nettles: Banishing and Binding.
Nutmeg: Healing.
Oak: Healing and Strength.
Oak Moss: Wisdom.
Oats: Prosperity.
Olives and Olive Leaf: Spirituality and Healing.
Onion: Banish negative energy.
Orange: Energy and Friendship.
Pansy: Mental clarity and Memory.
Papaya: Women's issues.
Parsley: Lust and Sex for a spouse.
Passion Flower: Relieves stress and Stabilizes loves.
Patchouli: Lust and Sex for a spouse.
Peach: Heartbreak.
Pear: Loyalty.
Pecan: Employment issues.
Peony: Friendship.
Pine: Purifies and Success.

Pineapple: Friendship and Welcome.
Pomegranate: Knowing.
Potatoes: Truth Seeking and Warts.
Rose: Love.
Rooibos: Cleansing and Beauty.
Rosemary: Love and healing sex issues.
Sage: Cleansing.
St. John's Wort: Happiness and Gratefulness.
Sandalwood: Consecration.
Star Anise: Blessings and Prosperity.
Strawberry: Love.
Sunflower: Energy, Thanksgiving and Friendship.
Sweetpea: Kindness and Friendship.
Thyme: Healing and Binding spells/prayers.
Tomato: Sex issues.
Tulip: Friendship.
Turmeric: Healing.
Valerian: Managing anxieties.
Vanilla: Magical energy.
Violet: Love.
Walnuts: Nervous system issues and fertility.
Wheat: Prosperity and Thanksgiving.
Willow: Healing and Wisdom.
Wormwood: Knowing and Beauty.
Yarrow: Love, Protection and Beauty.
Ylang Ylang: Lust and Sex in marriage.

Color Energy Chart

Black: Black is the color of power for magical purposes, used for candles, ribbons, and strings, etc… Black is the culmination of the absorption of all the colors. This is a color that energizes and stabilizes if worn as clothing. Black in the aura (bio-electric energy field of all living things) can signify that there is an imbalance of energy, and that the energy field of the body is trying to compensate by "sucking" lots of energy into itself.

Brown: Brown is the color of grounded magical energy with the deep earth for candles, etc.... It is a stabilizing color and a patient color when worn as clothing. Brown in the aura can signify a recent contact with the earth through gardening and planting, or through meditations regarding earth energy.

Red: Red is the color of passion and fire for magical purposes. When worn as clothing the vibration brings fierce energy and strength. Red in the aura can signify anger, great passion or a fierceness of beliefs, or can signify good, solid self-esteem if located in the hip area.

Orange: Orange is the color of creativity for magical purposes and is very vibrant and energizing when worn as clothing. Orange found in the aura can signify emotional stability and generosity and healthy digestive system if found in the middle stomach and lower back region. If muddy orange, there is possibly over-indulgence and selfishness involved in this person's life and may be affecting their digestion.

Yellow: Yellow is the color of joy and air for magical purposes. When worn as clothing, yellow can attract transformation and a sense of happiness. If found clear and shining in the solar plexus area, the person is often happy and easy-going. If mucky or dull, there may be an issue of abuse in this person's life, or possible addiction issues.

Green: Green is the color of plants and trees and represents the element of earth for magical purposes. When worn as clothing, it connects your energy to the surface energies of the earth and all living foliage. If found clear and bright in the area of the heart, then the person is probably well aware of earth issues and is considered "green". A clear color in this area also represents a healthy heart and circulatory system. If mucky or clouded, the emotional systems may be out of balance and causing circulatory and gastric problems.

Blue: Blue is the color of water, fidelity, and healing for magical purposes. When worn as clothing, it signifies loyalty and royalty, especially when bright, and signifies a healer when light colored. If found clear and bright in the neck area of the aura, the person has clear communication skills and knows oneself very well, which brings natural confidence. If dull or blocked, then the person might need help expressing himself or herself and may be emotionally abused or severely "stressed out."

Indigo: Indigo is a very dark blue color and is the color of perception and knowing for magical purposes. When worn as clothing, it signals a solid character and mind. When found solid and clear in the aura at the brain area, it might mean that the person is intelligent and mentally balanced, possibly very intuitive of people and situations. If dull or mucky, it may mean that the person does drugs or is being manipulated in some way.

Violet/Purple: Purple is the color of spirituality and wisdom for magical purposes, and is associated with the element of spirit. When worn as clothing, it signifies a spiritual journey and even marriage and is also a color of royalty. When found clear and bright in the aura at the top of the head, the person is connected to God, may be "Psychic" and is growing in their spiritual path. If muddy looking or dull in color, this person may not have yet found the Lord and is struggling with themselves and the meaning of life. They may be somewhat depressed.

Grey: Grey has a neutral frequency in magical energy and lacks devotion or passion. When worn as clothing, it fades the person's personality and blends them in with their surroundings, a good color choice of you're going for "invisibility". If found in the aura in any area, it signifies possible disease, physical or psychic attacks and spiritual oppression or spiritual lack of fulfillment. Grey is the color that can signify a pollutant and a dulling of the aura energies from internal or external sources. This is a color in need of deep healing.

White: White is the magical color of truth, innocence and purity, reflecting all the other colors. When worn as clothing, it signifies a peacefulness and harmony. A white aura is reached by the energy of the body matching, integrating with, and amplifying all the other energies. Varying degrees of this "shining" are observed throughout people and nature. This type of extreme light is referred to in Christian circles as the "Shakina Glory"; and is found Biblically with Moses, Elijah, Jesus, and the Angels. It is said that God is so bright, that we as humans are not able to even look upon Him.

Crystal Energy/Conductivity Chart

Amber: Magical energy flow and manifestation. Breaking hexes and healing.

Amethyst: Transmuting negative energy into positive energy. Protection and spirituality.

Bloodstone: Healing, Courage and Integrity.

Carnelian: Success at work, Grounding and Personal Power.
Citrine: Mental acuity, Prosperity.
Coral: Calming and Protection.
Diamond: Amplifies energy. Strength.
Emerald: Truth, Wisdom, Artistry/Creativity.
Garnet: Balances energies. Devotion.
Hematite: Balances and flows natural energies.
Herkimer Diamond: Relieves stress, Balances natural power grids.
Iron Pyrite: Wealth and Honesty in business dealings.
Jade: Harmony and Friendship.
Jasper: Gathers and Grounds energy.
Jet: Bends natural energies toward intention.
Lapis Lazuli: Knowing and Intuition.
Malachite: Strength, Prosperity and Focus.
Moonstone: Love, Comfort, Peace and Inspiration.
Onyx: Justice and Concentration.
Opal: Calming and Transforming of Energy.
Pearl: Softens natural energies.
Quartz Crystal (Clear): Draws, Stores, Amplifies and Projects energies.
Ruby: Self-Confidence, Intuition, Protection and Wisdom.
Sapphire: Wisdom, Material Gain, and Positive energy.
Sunstone: Healing and Success.
Tiger Eye: Truth, Confidence, and Protection.
Turquoise: Healing, Meditation and Communication.

Casting Template

Purpose:_____

Tools:_____

Herbs:_____

Candles:_____

Moon Phase:_____

Type of Casting:
Candle	Knot	Stitching	Cauldron
Circle	Potion	Powder	Ritual

Other:_____

Crystals:_____

Other Notes and Items:_____
_____

Prayer:_____
_____
_____
_____

Thoughts:_____

More "Witchy" Ways

Candle Magic

Candles are used in many worship rituals around the world, including Christianity and Wicca, making them a perfect media for Christian Witches. The connection of earth (wax), fire (flame), air (to burn), and water (in the wax and air), when combined with your spiritual energy, is a powerful way of casting a prayer.

Personally, I again combine the symbolic aspects of sympathetic magic, using color, symbols and phases of the moon. For example: If I want God to bless me with extra money, I choose a green candle to burn it on the full moon. First, I cleanse the candle and charge it with my own bio-energy. Then I usually carve it with symbols, names, or the desired outcome, something that serves to focus the energy that I'm putting forth into the prayer. I then light the candle, pray the prayer/spell and let it burn out. Here's some simple prayer candles to make for your self or as gifts for others.

Money Candle

Ingredients and Items: Something to carve with, a green votive or taper candle, lighter and suitable candle holder. Cleanse and charge all items.

To Do: Gather everything and caste a circle. Carve the green candle with a dollar sign, yen sign, pound sign or whatever sign of money you are used to while visualizing the money in your mind. Concentrate on money and put the candle in the holder as you light the wick and pray:

God send money unto me,

And harming none, Lord, meet my need. Amen.

Repeat the prayer until you feel sure that God hears you. Thank God for His results, whatever they may be in this matter. Release the circle and let the candle burn down.

Mending a Relationship Candle

Ingredients and Items: Something to carve with, a white votive or taper candle, lighter and suitable candle holder. Cleanse and charge all items.

To Do: Gather everything and caste a circle. Carve the white candle with a 'stitching' design, or the name of yourself and whomever you want to make up with, while visualizing this person's face. Concentrate on the person as you put the candle in the holder, light the wick and pray:

Father God, please help me mend,

The faith and love restore again.

Between us sew the open tear,

And heal us both with loving care. Amen.

Repeat the prayer until you feel sure that God hears you. Thank God for His results, whatever they may be in this matter. Release the circle and let the candle burn down.

Strength Candle

Ingredients and Items: Something to carve with, a red votive or taper candle, lighter and suitable candleholder. Cleanse and charge all items.

To Do: Gather everything and caste a circle. Carve the red candle with a cross and circle around it while visualizing mental, physical, or emotional strength in your mind. Concentrate on your personal strength and put the candle in the holder as you light the wick and pray:

Lord, my God, please lend your might,
To give me strength, both day and night.
Give me power, and it harm none,
Strengthen me for what's begun. Amen.

Repeat the prayer until you feel sure that God hears you. Thank God for His results, whatever they may be in this matter. Release the circle and let the candle burn down.

Knot Magic

Since weaving began, strings have been knotted with prayer, or so I'm told. No one has ever enlightened me about the actual history, but the Jews have worn tassels on their robes since before Jesus came in the flesh. There is even a Levitical commandment about the strings, so I feel very comfortable that knotting prayers into string is a very spiritual practice. For knot magic, I use the meaning of colors found in the chart section, and sometimes add scraps of cloth or very creative styles of knots.

When my son traveled Europe, his backpack had two white ribbons tied together in multiple knots with a prayer of protection spoken aloud for each knot. I knew the prayers would be heard, and honored. I also figured that in Europe, the simple presence of the knot, when recognized, would also help serve as a warning: This kid is magically protected. Yeah, I probably won't be getting the mother of the year award, but I do what I can.

I never told my son what this was all about, but knowing me and how I am, he knew there was something very special about those knotted up ribbons. So while on his travels, when he felt he needed a little extra blessing (also called "luck"), he would untie a knot. After returning home, he asked me about it and we had a good giggle about that weird ribbon thing!

There also came a time when I was creating a negative energy field around myself, and realized that I needed a little more forgiving of others in my life. It's amazing how I can forgive someone at communion, then turn around years later and pick that grudge up again. I am human, so to remind myself not to continue picking those angry feelings back up, I began knotting.

First, I wrote a list of all the people who I felt have wronged me on little slips of clothe. Then, taking a purple string, I began to tie the slips to the string with this prayer for each one:

I bind my anger and forgive,
_____ their sin against me,
So that I may live. Amen.

And the anger hasn't returned so far, but I hang the string on a private wall to remind me to stay in that forgiveness. I also left a long tail to add names on cloth in knots for the future.

Cauldron Magic

The traditional cauldron is a three-footed pot of varying sizes used in Europe since at least the 1500's. This iron pot was used for cooking, cleaning and dying of fabrics in the hearth of the kitchen, or out in open flame. This pot represented both the life giving womb of women, and the life-giving aspect of food. Cooking took time and a certain "watching" of the pot for the development of those hearty stews provided by God's grace and man's hard work. The cauldron was a tool at the heart of the home or village and was of great nurturing importance, so this traditional cauldron is a natural choice for the nurturing magics.

More modern cauldrons can still be made of cast iron with symbols upon them, made of brass or copper, with no feet, or can be as simple as a modern cooking pot and used on the stove top. Some are very fancy, with handles, carvings, stands, and room for candles beneath to warm the contents. And the contents are all symbolically matched to the intent of the prayer/spell. Please refer to the sympathetic and chart sections to create your own cauldron spells. Here's a simple cauldron spell of mine:

Loving Energy Home Cauldron Spell
Ingredients: Star Anise, Cinnamon, Clove and Rose Petals.
To Do: Fill the cauldron ¾ full with fresh water and add the following in sequence while praying and stirring Doesil with a wooden spoon or wooden wand:
Star Anise to bless our home,
Blessings from God are free to roam.
Cinnamon to heal all past wounds,
Clove renews the Witch's, too.
Rose to promote the feelings of Love,
With hope and peace from the Lord Above.
As boiling and bubbling fills the air,
This home be filled with love, laughter and care.
As God wills…so mote it be!
Bring to a full, rolling boil, then turn down heat and let simmer until almost gone. I usually dispose of my cauldron contents in the north/west corner of my property, or give them back to the earth through the compost pile.

Stitching Magic

The wonders of creating beautiful and useful items as gifts, home décor, and magical items can be uniquely expressed in stitchery with color correspondence, symbols and even the actual stitching of prayer/spells. There are lots of types of stitching, from all around the world, and worth trying to see what you like.

I prefer embroidery, cross-stitch and sewing machine work (when the mood strikes), and have made book covers, table clothes, "runners", alter clothes, bags, pillows, coasters, just tons of fun and special stuff.

The key to this type of magic is again, concentrating and focusing energy into the stitches and the creation of the item. You can pray with each stitch, each row, each individual object, even charming the object upon completion for a specific purpose. As an example, I have included the following:

Peaceful Dreams Pillow

Ingredients: 2- 5 x 5 pieces of white cross-stitch canvas, 1 skein of violet embroidery thread, 1 embroidery needle, scissors, 1 cup lavender flowers, 3 feet violet ribbon (1/2 inch wide).

To Do: In the middle of one of the pieces of canvas, begin by stitching a cross. This can be a simple, or ornate cross, and you can get patterns from books, or make up your own. While stitching in this cross pray:

Lord, please protect the dreamer here,
Draw only dreams of peacefulness near.

When finished with the cross, begin stitching the 2 canvases together to begin forming the pillow. Start stitching at the top of the pieces, about 1 inch in from the edge. On the top line, while stitching to the right, pray:

With these stitches, bind in hope,
To this pillow, kindness note.

On the right side, while stitching to the right, pray:

With these stitches, bind in love,
To this pillow, soft as dove.

On the bottom side, while still stitching to the right, pray;

With these stitches, bind in joy,
To this pillow, peace employ.

Then stop, but do not tie the string off yet. Fill the pillow with the lavender, and then continue stitching while praying:

With these stitches, bind in faith,
To this pillow, "rest well," saith.

Then knot the thread at the end and trim. Take the ribbon and wrap three times around the middle and tie in a bow while praying:

Lord, please protect the dreamer here,
Draw only dreams of peacefulness near.
Grant the sleep that doth refresh,
And ensure a tranquil rest.
As God wills…so mote it be.

Keep this dream pillow under your regular pillow in bed for peaceful dreams and a refreshing sleep.

Touch Magic

Touch magic takes the concept of "charging" an item to a whole other level. Touching with energy can both heal and harm and even change the cellular structure of an object. Remember when I was teasing about splitting open a tree? This is the concept I was referring to.

Energy can never be destroyed, just changed from one form into another and moved around, gently or with great force. If you get good at this "moving" of energy, you can manipulate it toward the benefit of all in many circumstances, as long as God allows you to. This is Key: As long as God allows you to. Remember, His will, not just ours.

To begin moving energy, start pulling the earth, air, fire, or water energies through your extended left hand. Breathe deeply, in your nose and out your mouth. Control your breathing and stay calm. Allow your shoulders to relax. Visualize the element being drawn gently in through your palm and wrapping around your spine.

Your palm should grow warm, there should be a strange sensation moving up your arm and you should feel the warmth and strange sensation moving down through your spine and up toward your neck. When it reaches up your neck and just below your head, stop pulling in the energy. If you don't stop, you will have one bad headache. So when the warmth reaches your neck, slowly extend your right hand and begin to "push" the energy gently back out the palm. You can "push" this energy into anything, or let it quietly go back to the earth for recycling. Practice this as often as you can throughout the day, and with the different elements. If you are left-handed, then pull with the right and release with the left.

Eventually, as your body grows more accustomed to manipulating these elemental energies, you will be able to mix them together and hold more and more energy around your spine.

If you do take in too much energy and grow a headache, immediately hold a clear quartz crystal in your right hand, pointed away from you and begin pushing the energy out and down to the ground. Remember to breathe naturally in through your nose and out your mouth. Do not panic.

When the energy surge subsides, relax your shoulders and stretch your neck. Imagine your hips and feet growing down into the ground as deep roots like a tree. This is called grounding and is a useful tool for any time you feel "off". If you still have a headache, try drinking a cup of Stress Reliever Tea.

When you grow comfortable with drawing and releasing energy, begin "holding" it in your spine, storing it for future release into people for healing, objects for "charging", things you create, prayer/spells and for self-defense. Never use this energy to overpower others or manipulate them for selfish means…only for physical self-defense. This is a martial art principle and works within the will of God.

Warning: If you "pull" energy from another living thing or person, there are spiritual and moral issues involved, and with people, you will be taking the chance of pulling in any nasty spirit or unbalanced energy (disease) that they may have, too.

Touch magic is also called "laying on of hands." You can push this extra energy into people, plants, animals and trees, thus helping provide them with more energy for God's healing. Again, these are the energies that come from what God has already established (the elements). We are not "Holy Ghost Channelers" with the Holy Spirit at our beck and demand.

I do not recommend allowing yourself to pull energy from any spirits, angels or other beings or allow them to posses your body and use it in any manner. You can never be sure what energy you're getting from them, as there are many lying and manipulative spirits, especially demons that will try to convince you that they are the "holy spirit". Besides, the real Holy Spirit in all "saved" Christians does not appreciate the company.

Drawing Down the Moon

There are probably as many ways to "Draw Down the Moon" as there are witches and covens (traditional groups of witches that gather together regularly for formal ritual). But for me, drawing down the moon, means pulling the moon energy into my body for healing and future use.

This is a different energy, and as it comes into my left hand, it feels cool and magnetic. I lift my left hand toward the moon and concentrate directly on the moon with my eyes and body until the moonbeams begin to literally streak down to my hand. My hand begins to softly glow a kind of bluish color, and the energy gently swirls around my arm and into my spine, then over and through my body. This is one energy that seems not to give me a headache as it travels and stays. This could be because moon energy has a very definite female frequency, and I am very definitely female.

Moon energy is very soft and calming, and is good to use in the healing of "hot" diseases, such as fever, emotional angers, cancer and allergies. It is also very effective in assisting the work of personal transformation of any kind and when working with children. I even leave my moon stone jewelry out overnight in the full moon because these crystals naturally gather and store the moon's energy.

Drinking in the Sun

Sun energy is both warming and regenerating. It is useful in healing "cool" diseases, such as depression, colds and flu, and some joint and muscle pains and bone degenerative illness or breaks. To gather this energy, I lay out in the sun during the midday when, in the desert, it is not to hot. When it does get too hot, I go back inside…but that's just me. Because this energy is so very powerful, it is important to wear sunscreen if you lay out to block some of these rays. They are so powerful that they will burn you if you stay in them directly for to long.

It's also very important to balance the major energy of the sun by drinking lots of water, especially if you are a woman. The water calms and disperses this vibrant energy throughout our cells and stores it for healing use, as the sun's energy has a definite male frequency. As with all living things, we cannot heal or thrive without the "male fertilization" of the sun's rays, which also gives some of the vitamins that are necessary for life.

More Prayer/Spells

Note: Keep in mind that all spells/prayers are more effective when you make them yourself. Following are more examples that you can change, use as written, or use as an inspiration for your own crafting. Always let the Holy Spirit guide you...Blessed Always Be!

This prayer/spell was written and cast for a dear friend of mine, and the words flowed easily, inspired by the Holy Spirit. After I cast it, this person's outlook and circumstances changed for the better. All praise and glory be to God!

Home Blessing
Ingredients: Rose water in a spritzer/sprayer and anointing oil.
To Do: Spritz the rose water throughout the home while praying:
Please bless this home, oh Ancient of Days,
And fill it with your loving ways.
Cleanse the space and make it glow,
Your love and light to clearly show!
Anoint the doors and windows with the oil while praying:
Bless the floor and walls and roof,

To comfort us and offer girth…
Protection from the evil ones,
Abides with thee, within our home!
Amen.

"Restore the Energy" Balance Spell

(If someone with a negative attitude has entered your home environment by invitation and they need help adjusting.)

Ingredients: The absorbed elements of earth, air, water and fire into your body.

To Do: Cast a circle of light, push the elemental energy into the sphere while praying:
Erase all curses and evil eye,
Destructive energy away now fly!
Change dark thoughts and shadows sent,
To love and light, of darkness repent!
Until the love of peace is learned,
Stop this nastiness, with love returned!
All curses cast are now removed,
The damages done to now improve!
In light and love I humbly ask,
Reset this balance and ease this task!
In God of peace and harmony…so mote it be, so mote it be!
Release the circle and smile.

The Halloween "Letting Go" Ritual

(AKA: The Morgan spell.*This spell utilizes the thinning of the veil to banish past hurts and pains inflicted by others throughout the year or years, sending the energetic "baggage" away for God's recycling, but can be adapted for any time of the year.)

Ingredients: Rainbow Obsidian, 5 white pillar candles, list of past hurts and betrayals, anointing oil, cauldron and a lighter, Lavender/rose/salt mixture to add to a cleansing bath or to the bottom of your shower for immediately after the ritual.

To do: Anoint your hands and forehead with the anointing oil. Cast the circle of protection with the candles. Put the stone somewhere on your person (jewelry or in pocket). Raise white light energy within the circle. Burn the paper (list of past hurts, etc.) and drop into the cauldron while praying:

Retain the knowledge to Wisdom's will,
Release the anguish that haunts my still.
All the anger and all the fears,
That I've collected through the years…
I push it to the great beyond,
For God to bless through sacred song.
It is my will to let it go,
New life begins with loving glow.
So mote it be!

Release the energy and the circle and thank God. Proceed to the shower or bath and add the salt/rose/lavender. Let the water wash away any clinging negative energy and surround yourself with white light. Don't "call back" your baggage.

*Morgan is a 5 lb. poodle with a painful past, who was very eager to participate in this ritual.

Thieving Key Spell

(Protects home and family from thievery, both overt and covert.)

Ingredients: A set of keys (real or fake) and a red ribbon.

To do: Take the keys and touch all the doors of your home while praying each time:

Oh Father God….

With this key, lock out thieves in the light,
With this key, lock our thieves in the night.
In Jesus name...so mote it be.

Tie up the keys with the red ribbon and hang them over the front door.

A "Deep Struggle" Prayer for Another

Ingredients: 4 small white votive candles, 1 pink taper candle, candleholders, lighter and a copy of the prayer with name filled in.

To do: Place the 4 white candles on a table in a North, South, East, West alignment, and the taper in the middle. Caste a circle and begin praying:

Oh, Father, grant the following things,

Your love to guide on Holy Wings.

Strength of Air, your joys to sing, (Light the eastern most candle.)

Let _____ serve our Christ, the King.

Strength of fire, for _____'s heart, (Light the southern most candle.)

Ignite the Spirit, faith impart.

Strength of Water, buoyancy float, (Light the western most candle.)

Hope among _____'s challenges mote.

Strength of Earth, to ground _____'s mind,

(Light the northern most candle.)

Peace in struggling let him/her find.

These things I pray as living keys,

And as thy will...so mote it be. (Light the center taper candle.)

In Jesus, Amen.

Release the circle and thank God for His divine wisdom and perfect will.

Clarity of Problem Candle

Ingredients: Something to carve with, a white votive or taper candle, lighter and suitable candle holder. Cleanse and charge all items.

To do: Gather everything and caste a circle. Carve the white candle with two "wavy" lines, while visualizing the problem, as you understand in now in your mind. Concentrate on the problem and put the candle in the holder as you light the wick and pray:

God Above, please help me know,

The answers to this puzzle grow.

Help me, Lord, to understand,

The answer in this troubled land. Amen.

Repeat the prayer until you feel sure that God hears you. Thank God for His results, whatever they may be in this matter. Release the circle and let the candle burn down.

Bless and Bind an Evil Enemy

Ingredients: Glass jar with lid, Paper with the name of the person on it in black ink. Mortar and Pestle. Garlic, Blessed Thistle, Stinging Nettle (Dry), Sea Salt, Sage. A little crooked stick that will fit in the jar. Sealing wax (or candle wax), lighter and seal (if you have one.) String, ribbon or raffia. Small clear quartz crystal that will also fit in the jar. Consider "Witchy" background music to increase concentration. And five white pillar candles for the circle.

To do: On a full moon: Gather, cleanse and charge ingredients and tools. Take a bath and imagine God surrounding you in warm and white light, letting any gray muck from your aura wash away down the drain and back to the earth.

Cast a circle with the candles (please refer to circle casting section). Place the name in the bottom of the open jar and begin praying:

God of All, Ancient of Days,
Keep me in your wisely ways.
_____ is causing damage and harm,
And spiritual warfare has been born.

Place the name in the jar with the little crooked stick. Gather the herbs into the mortar and pestle as follows while praying:

With this Nettle, now I bind _____ within a hedging vine,

With this Sage, asking God to cleanse,

the damages done to my family and friends,

With this Garlic, the bind grows stronger, until this evil is no longer.

With Blessed Thistle, I now request, the Spirit change and bless this bound guest.

The salt to seal and sanctify, this binding lock be not defied.

Grind the ingredients in the Doesil direction and when ground, pour into the jar. Adding the crystal pray:

With this quartz to now ensure, this blessing and binding in strength occurs.

Put the lid on the jar and wrap the string around it while praying:

I bind you _____ from harming that which is light,
I bind you _____ from harming that which is light,
I bind you _____ from harming that which is light!

As God wills…so mote it be!

Seal with the wax, thanking God for His will, and release the circle. Bury the jar at a cross roads or corner of your property.

Create a Harmonious Home

Ingredients: Cauldron and wooden spoon or wooden wand. 1 Small jar that will seal, with the lid. Angelica, Catnip, 1 Pear, Nutmeg, Clove Essential Oil, 1 Orange, 7 Sunflower Seeds. Water.

To do: Clean your home...not intimidatingly spotless (unless this is really you), but make sure it's reasonably clean. Fill cauldron ¾ full with water and begin to simmer. Caste a circle of light and begin humming your favorite song. While you are humming, add the ingredients separately and deliberately, while visualizing happy memories of your family, and how you want your home to be. Stirring Doesil with the spoon or wand, pray:

My Father God, you do know me...
Help me create a home of joy and safety!
I'll do the work, and change my ways,
Thanking you for every day!
I love you, God, and hope you find,
This household in your light divine! Amen.

Continue stirring the mix for a while, and then release the circle. Let the cauldron simmer, then put a little of the mixture that is left in a small bottle. Fill it to the top and put on the lid to seal. Dispose of the rest properly. Set your little jar in the kitchen window and begin working on your personal issues that will ensure the creation of a happy home.

Protect a Furry Friend

Ingredients: 1 small medallion (tag) with your name, phone number, and the animals name on it. 1 Collar (black or white.) Olive Oil, Lavender Essential Oil, and Cedar Wood Essential Oil.

To do: Mix 1 Tablespoon Olive Oil, 3 Drops Lavender Oil, and 3 Drops Cedar Wood Oil together. Rub some of this oil onto your hands, then hold the tag, and while rubbing, pray:

God Above, please charm this bauble,
Protect my friend from harm and trouble.
Keep them safe and in your light,
Protect my friend both day and night!
As God wills...so mote it be.

Wash your hands. Attach the tag to the collar, and then to your friend. Repeat and replace as needed.

Joy Candle

Ingredients: Something to carve with, a yellow votive or taper candle, lighter and suitable candle holder. Cleanse and charge all items.

To do: Gather everything and caste a circle. Carve the yellow candle with a smile, while visualizing bubbly laughter coming from you. Concentrate on the feeling of joy and put the candle in the holder as you light the wick and pray:

Father bring the laughter 'round,
The sounds of joy and fun abound.
Let this candle shine your laughter,
Bringing joy for ever after. Amen.

Repeat the prayer until you feel sure that God hears you. Thank God for His results, whatever they may be in this matter. Release the circle and let the candle burn down.

Bless a Garden

Ingredients: 9 quartz rocks of clear, white, or pink color. And of course, a garden.

To do: Stand in a clear spot of the garden. Visualize yourself covered in white light, and then visualize the garden growing profusely and thriving with good bugs and critters. Begin building a "spiral" of the rocks that begins at the outside edge of the spiral and continue placing the rocks in a doesil direction to the center. As you place the center stone, let the energy of the sun and moon flow from your right hand and into this stone. Pray:

Bless this garden to grow and prosper,
Protect from blight and feed our hunger.
Give the critters balance, too,

For all living things belong to you!
As thy will...so mote it be.

Leave the stones in place, tend the garden and enjoy! Remember to thank the plants for all cuttings and thank God for all the results.

Bless a New Home

Ingredients: Besom, Pint of water and Pint of salt. Spray bottle.

To do: Mix the salt and water in the spray bottle and charge with your energy and set aside. Starting at the front door, begin "sweeping" with your besom all through the rooms in a doesil direction while praying:

Stir up the energy within this home,
Bring in the good to freely roam.
Life and love and energy,
Of joy and fun now let there be!

Then take the spray bottle and begin spraying in the corners of all the rooms, again in a doesil direction, and pray:

God of All, please bless this space,
And fill it with your holy grace.

When you have been through every room, pour the rest of the salt water out on the ground just outside the front door, or if you have a porch, where you will be entering the home the most.

Charmed Hair Ties for a Little Girl

Ingredients: Lavender Essential Oil, Water, a medium sized Bowl, Scissors or (if you are a gardener) the Knife you use for harvesting in the garden, and 3 feet each of ribbons in these colors: Red, Orange, Yellow, Green, and Blue.

To do: Caste a circle. Take the ribbons and put them all together with the ends even. Cut the ribbons in half and set them aside in two even piles...one to the left side of your work area, and one to the right.

Taking the bundle on the left, hold it in your hands and charge while praying:
Ancient of Days, I follow the ways,
Of brightest blessings and magical days,
Charming these ribbons with glory of love,
Please bless this child with light from above.
As God wills...so mote it be!
Tie the ribbon bundle with one knot in the middle. Repeat for the right side bundle. Release the circle and use these ribbon bundles for ponytails, and braids.

Reverse the Curse Spell

Ingredients: 1 White Candle, Candle holder and a Lighter. Rosemary oil.

To do: Gather the ingredients and cast a circle of light. Anoint you palms and soles of your feet with the oil. Light the candle and pray:
Father God in Heaven Above:
Reverse the curse, or nasty spell...
Send it away, but graceful tell...
Thrice to thrice the blessing teach...
Reverse the spell from evil's reach.
Negate the darkness, replace with light...
No back reversal or further fight.
Please teach the curser love and peace...
Reverse the spell, and cast it from reach.
As thy will...so mote it be.

Release the circle and let the candle it burn out. Remain completely silent about casting this spell.

Witch's Bottle for Household Blessings

Ingredients: 1 heart shaped bottle with a stopper. Herbs: Rosemary, Lavender and Sage.

To do: Gather the ingredients and cast a circle of light. Add the herbs to the jar, then charge between your hands while praying:
Rosemary's loving and
Lavender's kind...
Sage is for healing,
And blessings abide...
I charge now this bottle and
Seal it with power...
May God bless this household from this very hour.
Amen.
Release the circle and place the bottle in the kitchen windowsill or by the main entrance into your home.

Spring Blessings Cauldron Spell

Ingredients: Cauldron and water with wooden spoon or wooden wand. Herbs: Lemon balm, Lavender, Ginger, Peppermint, White Willow Bark.

To do: Gather the ingredients and cast a circle of light. Add the herbs to the cauldron while stirring doesil and praying:
Lemon balm for kindness,
And Ginger for passion,
Willow for health,
And sunshine's the fashion!
Peppermint for riches that come from above,
I boil this cauldron with laughter and love!
If God doth will this blessing for spring,
With glory and harmony...so mote it be!
Release the circle and let the cauldron boil down. Pour the remains in your yard or compost pile.

Poetry

Deflation to Peace
Let the world go on without me,
Sand castles on the waves…
The narcissistic religions,
And taxes on our days.
Give me simple, Give me God,
And waxing moon and sun…
The glade, the dell,
The ones I love…
Enough for anyone.
—H. Fuller Hutchinson

The Moonlight Sisterhood
I call upon the Diety,
Of perfect love…so mote it be!
I am the daughter of the light,
Shining forth in darkest night!
As above…be now below,
My spirit shines with loving glow!
To know, to will, to dare and keep silent,
I am the gifted who keeps quiet!
I keep the magic through space and time,
Casting my pearls in the life divine!
I am the sister of moonlight,
Magic beacon shining bright!
—H. Fuller Hutchinson

Praise
Holy Spirit filled with power,
Reside in me in every hour.
With power to heal and power to bind,
Keep my in your love sublime.
Give me wisdom with your touch,
Protect me in the grace of Jesus.
—H. Fuller Hutchinson

Working with Others

Depending on the group, whether it is a formal coven, a circle of friends, or a general social gathering, there are nuances of "manners" that should be respected. For example, it is very bad manners to reach out and touch someone's jewelry, Book of Shadows, alter, charms, bottles and bags or magical tools and supplies without asking permission. Don't be offended if the answer is a "no, please don't touch..." as often these items are charged for a specific purpose and don't need your bio-energy mucking it up. It's not an insult, but an issue of respecting each other's magic. Just because it glows, doesn't mean you should touch it.

Same goes with people...don't touch without permission, no matter how innocent the touch may be. And protect yourself with a strong white light when other's attempt to touch you, politely asking them not to. For those of us who are big huggers, this is not a hard, fast rule, but it is always wise to be careful. Touch is a transfer of energy, whether welcome or not, and may get you in spiritual trouble of all kinds. So be careful about who you touch, and who you allow to touch you.

It is bad manners, and worse yet, unethical, to cast upon anyone in any way without their full knowledge and permission, except in cases of defense, protection, and extreme circumstance. When blessing a person or household humbly ask for permission to do so, and you will often be welcome back!

I also suggest that you be very clear about your own belief system to avoid any misunderstandings as to what kinds of magic you create and will be allowed to participate in. In our position, as Christians, who are witches (notice I put the Christian description first). There is often confusion in the first place that needs to be cleared up.

One of my dearest friends was very surprised to discover that I am first a believer in Christ, and not some sort of a hybrid Wiccan who believes that Jesus was just a great teacher and magician here on earth. Even though, from the start, I described myself as a Christian, proclaimed the good news of the Messiah (including the God with us part), and was very clear that any of my 'readings' and healing herbal magic came directly from God, his interpretation of that was based from his own background as a Wiccan Priest and Shaman. We got further into this issue, and he now describes me as a woman of faith. This is a great compliment. So consider the power of faith when working with others, try and see where their mindset is coming from. Understand that they probably don't see the width and breadth of your belief system unless you are very clear and direct, just as you won't see theirs, unless you listen and inquire.

Along that wave of thought, it is also very wise to explain to people why you won't be participating in calling upon other spirits, worshiping another god or goddess, or other things that go against your faith. If you do this with love and compassion (not aggression or a will to change the other person), this can both gain you respect as a strong Christian and help keep you safe from those witches and Christians who are interested in exploiting you.

I once attended a monthly social gathering of magical people.

After enjoying the fellowship for a couple of times, a new witch attended the gathering and began her "uber-witch" shenanigans. For those of you who don't know yet, "uber-witch" shenanigans are the actions, words and behaviors designed to let everybody know that this witch is far superior and more powerful in every way than anybody else in the group or in any given room. Sure signs of the "uber-witch" are: Talking down to others, monopolizing the conversations, positioning his or herself at the alter, displaying not-requested demonstrations of hypnosis or other "special" powers they possess, lots of "credentials" that they are more than happy to brag about, and general pushiness, even to the point of coercion. Stay away from these people, they are up to no good and will exploit you any time they can.

So anyway, she was bound and determined to hold a very public gathering of pagans here in our town (pushily, loudly and boisterously) and promptly began to organize us all into joining her cause. I, of course, did not join in her enthusiasm or her drive to mobilize us under her authority…so I remained quiet. Eventually, she point blank asked me in front of many of the others if I would be joining them in this endeavor. I very nicely replied, "No", and was willing to leave it respectfully at that. She, of course, promptly demanded that I explain why I wouldn't support this. Having been put on the spot, I responded that "I am not a pagan." Luckily, there were a lot of very studied and respectful magical people in this group that supported my decision, instead of feeling alienated themselves. A few even chuckled out loud. So be very clear and respectful, speaking the truth in kindness and strength.

Working with others can be fun and very powerful, but as with all groups, magical people come with personalities, issues, and unfortunately, they can also come with personal agendas for self gratification. Beware of the covens and any witches who practice public pressure, and especially those who encourage or demand entrance into a "hive" or "group" mind.

Following is an outline for an informal Christian Witch's coven, or a more formal Christian Witch's circle of friends.

Christian Witch's Circle

Group Standards

1. Only Christian Witches will be allowed to join the group.
2. Never use magic for evil. Do not attempt to usurp the will of God.
3. Honor and respect all. Do not abuse, manipulate, control or cast against the group.
4. Do everything you do in life to the best of your ability. Do not live your life or practice magic slovenly or maliciously.
5. Keep the groups' secrets. We are Christians and should live with loyalty and kindness.

Code of Conduct

1. Members of this group will follow these codes to the best of their ability:
2. Always try to use appropriate manners. No cussing, swearing, etc....
3. Use discression in all matters. Do not be loud and boisterous, but joyful and encouraging.
4. Do not abuse. Treat people with as much respect as possible.
5. Fairly take and fairly give. Do not take advantage of others, and do not allow them to take advantage of you.
6. Follow the Christian Witch's Rede as closely as possible.

7. Take care of yourself, your family, and your home to the best of your abilities.

Group Guidelines

1. Guidelines are established as voluntary group guidelines only and are not binding to liable through civil action by group or individual. Guidelines may be changed to reflect the changing of times and society. Guidelines may not be changed to embrace evil in any form or to enhance personal gain over each other and can only be changed by a majority vote of the group for the good of the group as a whole.
2. Membership is voluntary (no dues or fees unless supplies are provided/needed) and applicant will be voted upon after introduction of applicant (must be at least 21) to the group. Applicant will only be accepted into the group with a unanimous vote, and may be rejected for any reason. This is a lifetime membership unless asked to leave, or by choosing to leave for any reason. Individuals are fully accountable and responsible for themselves.
a. You will be asked to pay for your own supplies, books, and any other tools you may need to complete your training. Fees must remain "reasonable" for the member. You will not be charged for the actual teaching or verbal sharing of information and testing. You will also be expected to contribute to the gatherings, such as potluck, party supplies, time or talent, etc… No one is allowed to charge a group member fees for magical services or teaching of skills. Do not abuse this group.
3. Members may be asked to leave the group by majority vote for the following reasons:
a. Evil Magical Practices, "Stirring the Cauldron" with Nastiness, Gossip or Excessive "Drama", Failure to Contribute

Kindness and Support to the group, Serious Lapse of Morality, Complete Selfishness and Overt/Covert "Taking/Using," or betraying the secrets of the group, including exposing the anonymity of the members, especially those who are "in the broom closet."
b. Binding of oneself to a "Hive Mind/Group Mind/Energy Grid" type situation that may affect the group.
c. Purposefully allowing "possession" types of magic and mediumship, or calling up demons as "familiar spirits".
d. Controlling, Manipulating, "Infringing" Upon, "Spying" Upon, "Casting" Upon without consent, or otherwise abusing a member or the group.
e. Practicing Involuntary Hypnosis, hypnosis on an uninformed or poorly informed person (especially without witnesses/watchers), leaving behind unauthorized "suggestions" during hypnosis, or using NLP on others. This amounts to psychic assault and is a usurping of free will.
f. Abusing the clients that any member may acquire.
g. Copywriting, trademarking, registering, infringing upon, publishing, or copying or distributing without written and signed unanimous group authorization by the group of any of the materials created by the group including: Spells, Rituals, Teaching Materials, Books of Shadows, Skills Material, Video/DVD, CD, Photos or any other proprietary information belonging to the group. This is stealing, is illegal and is subject to criminal prosecution.
h. Exception: If you write and/or produce the original material yourself, it still belongs to you and you may distribute it as you see fit.
4. Meetings will be held spontaneously and occasionally and are not mandatory, but in keeping with the spirit of unity, should be participated in regularly. Visitors are not welcome unless they are

prospective members (applicants) and are expected by the other members at the group meeting.
5. These guidelines will be available to all potential members and will be understood and abided by all the members.

Skills and Teaching

Lessons can be taught by any member who has mastered the lesson. You may only teach what you have mastered, and have yourself been tested on. You must master all the skills in each level before moving on the next. The tests are both/either verbal exam and/or group demonstration. There are no time limits or pressure to develop your skills. You may add skills to the curriculum only after you have mastered all three levels. New skills may be added with complete materials only, and must be approved by majority vote to be taught to the group. The new skills will be added and presented in a seminar format to level three students only.

Level One: Becoming

Level one study and practice is designed to discover the magic that is within and to begin creating the magical life you desire. Level one provides the foundational basics for magical living.

Supplies: Books listed below.
            Book of Shadows.
            Alter items of your choice, to be purchased during this level.
Required Reading:
            The Holy Bible, New Testament.
            Witchcraft: A Mystery Tradition. Raven Grimassi.
            Meditation for Dummies. Stephen Bodian.

The Christian Witch's Handbook. H. Fuller Hutchinson.
The Magical Household. Cunningham and Harrington.
Earth, Air, Fire & Water. Cunningham.
Green Magic. Ann Moura.
Natural Witchery. Ellen Dugan.
The Magician's Companion. Whitcomb. Reference Book.
The Crystal Bible. Hall. Reference Book.

Skills & Tests:
1. Magical Theories and History
2. Magical Ethics and Manners
3. Book of Shadows: Hands-On Creation of Your Personal Magical Book.
4. Prayer & Meditation with Visualization
a. Warnings against Hypnosis, NLP and Transcendental Meditation
5. Laws of Magic: Web of Life, Sympathetic Magic, Threefold Law, As Above…So Below, Doctrine of Signatures. …and discussion.
6. Creating Magical Environments: Home, Alters, Gardens, etc…
7. Moon and Sun Energy & The Elements
8. Wheel of the Year: Basic Celebrations/Rituals
9. Other Celebrations and Rituals: Handfasting, Womanhood Rites
10. Magic 101:
a. Raising and Releasing Energy: The Elements (Pentacle), Circle Casting and Grounding, Charging and Cleansing (Basic Energy Techniques)
b. Correlations Charts: Phases of the Moon, Colors, Crystals, Herbs, Symbols, Oils, Flowers, Trees, Days of the Week, Months and Seasons

Level Two: Empowering

Level two study is designed to empower your magic to flow through practical application of magical knowledge and by developing your magical instincts. You will learn to create, write and cast spells through traditional methods and begin exploring the techniques of advanced energy manipulation.

Supplies: Books listed below.
Cauldron.
Basic herbs: Salt, Lavender, Rose, Angelica, Mandrake, Yarrow, Nettle, St. John's Wort, Garlic, Thyme, Rosemary, Clove, Peppermint, Bay Leaf, Sage.
Basic Oils: Lavender, Rosemary, Tea Tree, Ylang Ylang, Patchouli, Lemon, Peppermint, and a Carrier Oil.
Crystals: Rose Quartz, Clear Quartz, Amethyst Quartz.
Candles: 5 White Pillar, White, Red, Orange, Yellow, Green, Blue, Indigo, Purple (Tapers or votives.)

Section One Required Reading:
Kitchen Witchery. Daniel.
Encyclopedia of Natural Magic. Greer.
The Complete Book of Incense, Oils & Brews. Cunningham.
Magical Herbalism. Cunningham.
Charms, Spells & Formulas. Ray T. Malbrough.

Skills & Tests:
1. Creating spells: Goals and Ethics
2. Correlations and Media
a. Cauldron, Knot, Sachet (Bags), Candle, Stitchery, Cooking, Sculpting/Poppets, Painting, Bottles, Spatial, Potions (Teas/Oils), Powders, Incense/Aromatherapy, Other
3. Writing and Casting
a. Intent and Flow: Rhyming and Choosing words wisely
b. Protecting Yourself: Spheres of Safety
c. Circle Casting, Raising Energy, Spell Casting, Releasing

Section Two Required Reading:
Auras: See them in Only 60 Seconds. Smith

Energy Secrets. Alla Svirinskaya.
Hands of Light. Barbara Ann Brennan.
Skills & Tests:
4. Energy Work
a. Sound, Light and Subtle Bio-Energy Vibrations
b. Extra Sensory Perception, Aura and Chakra System
c. Collecting, Storing and Releasing Energy with your Body: Advanced Energy Techniques and Practice
d. Healing and Destroying: Manipulating Energy

Level Three: Specializing

Level three is the advanced application of magic and offers avenues of specialization and mastery, promoting continued practice, growth, education and exploration into the magical power that surrounds us all. Please choose at least one "specialty."

Supplies: Books and specialty items necessary for the completion of your specialty.
Prerequisite: Discuss and understand the ethics, legality and life as a "working" witch.
1. **Seer**: Accessing Information from the web of life. Required Reading: *The Gift: Echo Bodine. Trust Your Vibes:Sonia Choquette. The Art of the Pendulum: Cohen. The Art of Hand Reading: Lori Reid.*
a. Ethics and divination.
b. Connecting with the Divine. Warning against possession.
c. Focus Tools:
i. Arts: Cards, Stones, Pendulum, Black Mirror Scrying, Water Scrying, Psychometry
ii. Skills: Tea Leaves, Palm Reading, Candle Scrying
d. Understanding the information that comes to you: Visions,

Feelings, Sounds, Words, Symbols, Smells
e. Dreams
2. **Discerner:** Working with Spirits and Others. Required Reading: *Ghosts, Apparitions and Poltergeists: Brian Righi. When Ghosts Speak: Mary Ann Winkowski. Anything by John Edwards. Sixth Sense: Stuart Wilde.*
a. Ghosts
i. Theory, Encounter and Ethics
ii. Crossing Over, Banishing from a Space, Living With
b. Demons, Angels and Other Created Beings
i. Discerning and Appropriate Interaction
3. **Traveler:** Traveling Through the Worlds. *Sixth Sense: Stuart Wilde. The Dancing Wu Li Masters: Gary Zukav. Remote Viewing Secrets: Joseph McMoneagle*
a. Ethics and Traveling
b. Astral Projection (Flying)
c. Remote Viewing
d. Time Traveling
5. **Warrior:** Defensive Magic and Self-Defense. Required Reading: *The Witch's Shield: Penczak. Warrior of the Light: Paulo Coelho. The Art of War: Sun Tzu. Positive Energy: Judith Orloff. Buddhist Healing Touch: Yen, Chiang, Chen.*
a. Ethics and Emergency
b. Defensive Spells
c. Touch Defense: Energy Drain and Push
6. **Healer:** Practical Applications for Self-healing. Required Reading: *Family Herbal: Rosemary Gladstar. Prescription for Herbal Healing: Phyllis A. Balch. Energy Healing: Gilkeson. The Healer's Manual: Andrews. The Complete Book of Essential Oils & Aromatherapy: Worwood. Energy Medicine: Eden.*
a. Ethics and Healing
b. Energy Healing Techniques

c. Basic Herbalism and Aromatherapy
d. Ritual/Spell Healing
7. **Torchbearer:** Illuminator of deep occult knowledge, both white and black. Required Reading: *The "old testament" of the Bible Ritual Magic: What It Is & How To Do It: Donald Tyson. The Secret Teachings of All Ages: Manly P. Hall. Mythology: C.Scott Littleton. The Secret Doctrine: Blavatsky. The Celtic Book of Living and Dying: Juliette Wood* Lots of assorted Fairy tales…
a. Ethics and Sharing of Knowledge
b. Occult Practice, Ritual, and History
c. Lore and Legend

Casting the Circle of the Christian Witches

This circle is cast as a pentacle, with the top of the star facing northward. This circle is to raise elemental power and spiritual protection for the duration of the rituals, rites and initiations. It can be cast by a single person for oneself, for the group, or by 5 participants.

Begin by facing north and proclaim:
We call upon the Diety,
Of perfect love…so mote it be!
We call upon God, creator of spirit!
Moving to the right (Doesil) at the right point of the star proclaim:
We are the people of the light,
Shining forth in darkest night.
We call upon God, creator of water!
Still moving right, at the lower right point of the star proclaim:
As above…be now below,
Our spirits shine with loving glow!

We call upon God, creator of fire!
Continuing right, at the lower left point of the star proclaim:
To know, to will, to dare and keep silent,
We are the gifted who keep quiet!
We call upon God, creator of earth!
At the farthest left point of the star proclaim:
We keep the magic through space and time,
Casting our pearls in the life divine!
We call upon God, creator of air!
Again facing north proclaim:
We are the people of the light,
Magic beacons shining bright...
This circle now in love complete,
As is God's will...so mote it be!

To release the circle after the work is done, face the north and proclaim:
This circle whole is now released,
The will of God in love and peace!

Celebrations

The Christian Witch's Circle celebrates the four seasons together, including All Hallow's Eve, Yule, Beltane and Midsummer's Eve. Celebrations of the seasons are a family event, and all of the groups families are invited to attend.

All Hallow's Eve (October 31st)
This is the night of the turning of the year from life toward death, the male and female energies are balanced. The changing of the seasons turn from warm and sunnier to cold and darker. This is the night when the veil between the worlds is the thinnest,

and the spirits can easily cross over to earth, or from the earth to the heavens and otherworlds. This is the night that we celebrate the lives of those who have died through the ages and through the year.

This is the time for families, bonfires, treats, legends and ghost stories. It's great to dress as your favorite character (witch's included, of course!) It's fun to decorate, and celebrate this quintessential witch's holy day, when witches stand between the worlds.

The wreath: Straw or Grapevine.

The symbols of the season are: Pumpkins, Cauldrons, Besoms, and Spider webs.

The colors are: Orange, Purple, Green and Silver and Gold.

The herbal energies are: Bay Leaf, Lavender, Mugwort, Nutmeg, Sage, Ginger, Garlic and Mandrake.

The crystal energies are: Black Onyx, Bloodstone, Amethyst, Moonstone and Opal.

To do: Light candles for the dead, burn a bonfire and add incense to sooth any wandering spirits, carve jack-o'-the-lanterns, tell the stories and legends and have some fun!

Stories to tell: Jack stories, ghost stories, witch stories, legends of the "night creatures."

Prayers of Worship: This works well if everyone takes turns praying aloud with each other in the group.

Yule (December 21st)

The days are short and the earth is slumbering in her silvery moonlit night, beautiful and still. People are bustling and there's a general feeling of good will in the air. Yule celebrates the beginning of the turning of the year from death toward life. The seeds in the womb of the earth are preparing for spring, and the light will begin to return to the earth. This is the time of high female energy and the time of year for new beginnings and hopeful faith.

The wreath: Evergreen.

The symbols of the season are: Candles, Evergreen boughs, Evergreen Trees, Holly, and Mistletoe.

The colors are: Red, Green, White, and Gold.

The herbal energies are: Holly, Mistletoe, Pine, Cedar, Apple, Cinnamon, Oak, Chamomile and Sage.

The crystal energies are: Clear Quartz, Emerald, Pearl, Ruby and Sapphire.

To do: Decorate with evergreens, lights and a Yule Tree. Boil a cauldron of apple cider and cinnamon and charge with blessings for the coming year. Light a fire in the fireplace if you have one, then exchange gifts of promise and prosperity. Sing songs, read poetry, play games, feast on goodies and make merry!

Prayers of Worship: This works well if everyone takes turns praying aloud with each other in the group.

Spring (March 21st)

Spring is blooming out all over, and the fertility of the earth is showing. This is the time of fertility and birth. The sun is fertilizing the womb of the earth, and the new life is springing forth. Now is the time to fertilize the earth with new bulbs, enjoy the gardens, woods and waters, and welcome the spring rains. This is the night we find the excitement and balance between the male and female energies, and the fruit thereof.

The wreath: Flowers.

The symbols of the season are: Rabbits, Eggs, Flowers and Ribbons.

The colors are: White, Yellow, Cream, Green and Silver and Gold.

The herbal energies are: Rosemary, Roses, Mint, Ylang Ylang, Lavender and Patchouli.

The crystal energies are: Clear Quartz, Rose Quartz, Citrine and Amethyst.

To do: Plant new life together under the moon. Bake "witch cakes", decorate eggs, and dance under the stars and around the bonfire. Laugh, sing, and braid your hair with flowers.

Prayers of Worship: This works well if everyone takes turns praying aloud with each other in the group.

Midsummer's Eve (June 21st)

The longest day of the year, the male energies are at the strongest in full vitality and in the prime of life. This is the time of fairy kings, fairy tales and traveling between the veils of the otherworlds. Often considered the most magical time of the year, you may encounter strange happenings in the earth. Heroes and tales of old are born anew in legend and lore…and King Arthur tales abound in magic, mystery and joy.

The wreath: Ivy and Laurel.

The symbols of the season are: Green Man, Fairies, Glowing lights, Flowers, and Ivy.

The colors are: Green, Purple, Brown, Red, Blue, Gold and White.

The herbal energies are: Lavender, Wild Cherry, Horney Goat, Garlic, Horseradish, Rose and Snapdragon.

The crystal energies are: Bloodstone, Malachite, Smoky Quartz, and Ruby.

To do: Build a bonfire for the young to leap over for luck and prosperity, tell fairy tales and epic tales of heroes of old. Tell the tale of Jack Barleycorn, float candles in water, string glowing lights, wear flower garlands and enjoy!

Prayers of Worship: This works well if everyone takes turns praying aloud with each other in the group.

Group Casting

Spell casting by the group should be performed during a full moon, unless it's an emergency. The spell should be discussed and written in it's entirety before the casting, with all supplies necessary gathered and the goal decided upon in agreement.

Group Spells should contain the following aspects:

God should be acknowledged, asked and thanked.
All 5 elements should be represented.
Appropriate correlations should be included.
The goal and outcome should be thoroughly discussed and agreed upon.
Each person should contribute some aspect of the spell for optimal power and outcome. The basic format as follows:

Create the circle.
Cast the spell.
Release the circle.
Remain silent with others regarding the spell.
Add the spell to everyone's Books of Shadows with the date cast.

Christian Witch's Glossary

Aura: The bio-electrical field found surrounding all living things. May be visible to the human eye by those who are aware and sensitive to it.

Besom: A magical broom used for "sweeping" or otherwise moving natural energy.

Bio-energy: The natural energies and energy fields found in all creation. The form of natural living electrical charges.

Black Magic: Magic that is based in self-will and performed with an ultimately self-serving goal, whether it be for false worshipping, pseudo-healing, prosperity of the evil things, growth of the negative influences, or other. Black magic creates a spiritual void in the universe that contains neither light, nor darkness, but the total absence of light and natural life. For example: commanding and compelling spirits by your own will to do your bidding is definitely black magic.

Book of Shadows: The personal book of a witch that holds collections of magical information, spells and other occult knowledge.

Casting a Circle/Circle Casting: Creating a sacred spherical space of energy within which to perform magic, and/or to create a sacred sphere of protection.

Cauldron: A pot used for casting spells. Traditionally, cauldrons are three footed and made of iron.

Ceremonial Magic/Magician (Sorcerer/ess): One who practices the "commanding and compelling" of spirits through complex rituals based on the "self will" of the magician (witch). Some Wiccans also practice this direct form of ceremonial magic and some Christians practice this under the guise of "angel magic". This is considered a true form of sorcery.

Charged/Charging: To pass bio-energy into an object from ones self. When the bio-energy is transferred to the object, it is charged.

Christian: One who accepts Jesus the Christ as the Son of God, and God here on earth with us, sent to redeem our souls by the willful shedding of His blood on the cross, thus forgiving our sins, and allowing our souls the freedom to live in God's love and life forever. True Christians have a personal relationship with God and thus are children of the eternal light of love, and make every attempt to live accordingly, giving themselves over as servants to God's will. Unfortunately, many modern Christians practice a form of ceremonial magic by attempting to "command and compel" the Holy Spirit of God for their own use and ritual purposes.

Circle: A group of solitary witches who gather for learning purposes, sometimes "spell casting" and friendship. A circle is less formal and less structured in magical styles than a Coven and does not require a hive/group mind.

Coven: A group of witches who formally gather together for corporate worship and group rituals. Covens often have highly developed systems of conduct, with set styles of magic and complex rituals. Modern covens often include participation in a "hive" or "group mind".

Doesil: Any clock-wise motions, used to put energy into an object, ritual or spell.

Familiar (Witch's Familiar): A furry (or slimy) friend of a witch that may or may not choose to participate in spell casting with the witch.

Familiar Spirits: Angels, Demons, or Ghosts who communicate with a person. Spirit beings or beings with spirits from other realms. New Age theology often refers to familiar spirits as Spirit Guides. Biblical context is not spirits that you are familiar with (such as your dead uncle who visited before leaving for heaven) but those spirits whom a witch is cursed with, controlled by, or that the witch controls.

God (the Father): The Father aspect of the one true God, who is the creator and ultimate ruler of all that exists.

God (the Holy Spirit): The Mother aspect of the one true God, who indwells the Christian and empowers them to perform the will of God in their lives here on earth. Also called the Spirit of Wisdom, or the Spirit in the bible.

God (the Son): Jesus the Christ, the Son aspect of the one true God, who was born here on earth to redeem our souls from evil and eternal damnation.

Hedge Witch: A witch who specializes in the nature magics: herbs, trees, gardens, waters, etc... and the manipulation of these energies, often through the hands. Also, hedge witches often help to heal peoples' spiritual ailments through manipulation of bio-energy in the aura, seen as the working in the "hedge" between this world and others. Often a solitary practitioner.

Heritage/d Witch: A witch who has a lineage of magical knowledge from a magical tradition, or one who is a natural witch with other witches in their ancestry.

Hive/Group Mind: A ritual process that allows every member of a group to access the bio-energy of every other member of the group at any time, without clearly stated boundary or protection. This is sometimes done and often maintained through various types of group meditations involving crystals (crystal grid) or symbols established as THE focus tools for these group meditations.

This is a very potentially dangerous situation with some covens even allowing their "underlings" to absorb the negative energy that the "priest/ess" leaders may be experiencing under the guise of increased power, group protection and solidarity.

Kitchen Witch: A witch who practices magic primarily in the home, working with anything readily available at hand. Often a solitary practitioner.

Natural Witch: One who is born with the ability to manipulate natural energy. Can be a believer of any religious belief system.

NLP: Neuro-linguistic programming. A system of manipulating the human mind through applied touch and memory conditioning. Manipulates the mind/body consciousness.

Occult: Refers to "hidden" knowledge and sometimes to "magical" knowledge or practice. Not necessarily negative in connotation. All religions contain occult knowledge that is revealed with time and experience.

Ritual: An act of performing magic, with a repetitive nature, or a ritualized act of performing a spell. Also known as "ritual worship".

Solitary Practitioner: One who practices magic by themselves, and not within a formal coven.

Spell, Spell/Prayer or Prayer/Spell: The act of compiling words, actions, tools, elements, symbols and/or natural objects together into a ritual that manipulates bio-energy towards a desired outcome, such as healing, worshiping, etc... The Christian Witch does this as an act of serving God's will and often to petition God for change in a situation. Also known as casting a prayer.

Trinity: A theological concept that represents the three aspects of the one true God, as one God, and not a pantheon of gods. The trinity is often symbolized by a triune knot or "triskle". Also, this concept is repeated in the natural patterns of life, such as the three stages of womanhood: maiden, mother and crone; or the three stages of bounty: seed, plant and harvest.

Wand: A stick of wood, crystal, or some other substance used to direct bio-energy.

Wiccan: A magical practitioner (Witch) that generally follows a nature religion based in Western occult theological systems, called "Wicca." Wiccans often follow a pantheon of gods, which are expressed in many forms of a central god and goddess. Most also practice a form of ceremonial magic by compelling entities of the "watchtowers" during ritual work.

Widdershins: Any counter clock-wise motions, used to draw energy out of or to release energy from an object, ritual or spell.

White Magic: Natural magic that is based in the will of God and performed with love as the foundation, whether it is for worshipping, healing, protection, prosperity, growth, or other. White magic puts forth God's spiritual light into the universe through us and is creative, promoting life and God's will. For example: Christ using us to command and compel an evil spirit to leave a space or a person is white magic.

Witch: Any practitioner of the magical arts; one who may, or may not display psychic abilities. Also called a magician. Not necessarily a negative connotation.

Frequently Asked Questions

Isn't Christian Witch an oxymoron?
Not for me. A Christian is someone who believes in Jesus Christ as the redeemer of their soul and an aspect of the God they worship. A "Witch" is a magical practitioner, and not always an exclusive follower of the Wiccan religion. Wicca is another religion of itself, although they do practice magic, too. In other words, not all "Witches" are Wiccan.

Although I do believe in and practice many aspects of the Wiccan religion, I do not practice what has been called "Christian Wicca" because traditional Wicca, and what has been presented as "Christian Wicca" is based on worshiping a pantheon of Gods. In Christianity, there is only one God, with multiple aspects. These are mutually exclusive belief systems, although styles of worship can be similar, and is what I practice and have presented here.

What is magic, magick?
Magic (sometimes spelled "magick") is the manipulation of natural energies to provoke or enhance a desired outcome. This can include tools for focus, or items that contain energy themselves, such as: herbs, oils, candles, wands, words and symbols. People who are skilled at this are often called "Witches."

What about the Bible and magic?
The Holy Bible is the guidebook for humanity…or it should be, anyway. But the truth of the Bible is that it is a book, inspired by God, but not actually written by God. It was written by men who believed in God, and were inspired by various communications *from* God. The Bible will not "save your soul"…It is not a god, it is a book, written by flawed men and also compiled by flawed men into the "holy canon". And the Bible does not "say" anything…it is a book, not *the* Living Word, nor does it magically just start talking. Jesus is *the* Living Word.

However, the words and deeds of Jesus (who is God) were recorded by men into the "New Testament" and are historically verified by other sources of the period, a.k.a.: witnesses.

This book has often been misused to promote hatred and death among people, while Jesus promoted life, love, and liberty for the people. Quite frankly, I'll follow Jesus and who He is, and not a book. After all, this kind of a relationship with Him is what He died for.

What about the Church and magic?
The "Church" is supposed to be a living, breathing, evolving group of worshipers who love and/or are seeking the Lord God through the leadership of Jesus Christ. This is the perfect arena for God's magic: the people of the light.

The "Church" as Jesus described it is not a building, a hierarchy, or a social club. It is not the ultimate "judge" of how we are to behave and what we are supposed to believe. Jesus is.

Unfortunately, most western churches in America today seem to follow the Apostle Paul and his teachings, instead of Jesus Christ and His teachings. Or, they are often so busy "listening to" and "following a book" that they put that book ahead of the Spirit of God. I always want to ask: "Are we the people of the book, or the people of the Lord?" Worse yet, many proclaiming church members are using that book to justify their attempts of "spiritually murdering" their fellow man and especially their wives. You know who you are...

I, personally, would love to gather at a building weekly with believers in the Lord. Do you know where I can find one that isn't set up like a humanistic corporation with a marketing plan, board of directors, political agendas of personalities, and liability insurance? If you do, and it's not a cult, please contact me...I am not quite *that* jaded...yet.

If you would like to know more about magic *in* the church, you can research this online or at your local library.

Isn't magic and witchcraft evil?

No. Magic (the ability to manipulate natural energies) is not evil. This ability is naturally "born" into some people. For others, it is an acquired skill, and some say that everyone can do it. For even others, it is a scientific principle, for example: Quantum Physics...but no, magic is not evil. It's how you use it that makes the difference. "Witchcrafting" (crafting magic) should be used in agreement with the will of God, by people who are capable of it. People can be evil, spirits can be evil, but magic itself is not evil.

How do I become a Christian Witch?

Study about Jesus the Christ. Believe in Him as the redeemer of your soul, and your personal connection to God. Ask Him for forgiveness of your sins, and to lead you for the rest of your life. Study Him more, study about Him, and then study about magic. Create your personal relationship with Him...and you'll instinctively know when to perform magic through the Holy Spirit's calling to you. It's that simple...and that complex.

Brightest Blessings,
Hilea

Bibliography

Holy Bible. Various authors, translations and publishers.
Diane Ahlquist. *Moon Spells.* Adams Media Corporation. 2002.
Silver Ravenwolf. *Hedge Witch.* Llewellyn Publications. 2008
Gertrud Mueller Nelson. *To Dance With God.* Paulist Press. 1986.
Christopher Penczak. *The Witch's Shield.* Llewellyn Publication. 2006.
Rosemary Gladstar. *Rosemary Gladstar's Family Herbal.* Storey Books. 2001.
H.P. Blavatsky. *The Secret Doctrine.* Theosophical University Press. 1974.
Raven Grimassi. *Beltane.* Llewellyn Publications. 2001.
Marilyn F. Daniel. *Kitchen Witchery.* Weiser Books. 2002.
Scott Cunningham and David Harrington. *The Magical Household.* Llewellyn Publications. 2005.
Oberon Zell-Ravenheart. *Grimoire for the Apprentice Wizard.* New Page Books. 2004.
Unger's Bible Dictionary. Moody Press. 1967.
Manly P. Hall. *The Secret Teachings of All Ages.* Tarcher/Penguin. 2003.
Merril C. Tenney, general editor. *The Zondervan Pictorial*

Encyclopedia of the Bible. Regency Reference Library. 1976.

Robert L. Thomas, general editor. *The New American Standard Exhaustive Concordance of the Bible with Hebrew, Aramaic, and Greek Dictionaries.* Holman Bible Publishers. 1977.

Scott Cunningham. *The Complete Book of Incense, Oils, and Brews.* Llewellyn Publications. 2007.

Scott Cunningham. *Magical Aromatherapy: The Power of Scent.* Llewellyn Publications. 2006.

Ted Andrews. *The Healer's Manual: A Beginner's Guide to Energy Therapies.* Llewellyn Publications. 2007.

Ellen Dugan. *Garden Witchery* Llewellyn Publications. 2006.

Ellen Dugan. *Natural Witchery: Intuitive, Personal & Practical Magick.* Llewellyn Publications. 2007.

Barbara Ann Brennan. *Hands of Light: A Guide to Healing Through the Human Energy Field.* Bantam Books. 1988.

Judy Hall. *The Crystal Bible.* Walking Stick Press. 2003.

Phyllis A. Balch. *Prescription for Herbal Healing.* Avery. 2002.

Valerie Ann Worwood. *The Complete Book of Essential Oils & Aromatherapy.* New World Library. 1991.